Florida-Backroads-Travel.com

CENTRAL FLORIDA
BACKROADS TRAVEL

Second Edition, 2017

CONTENTS

Central

Ocala

MARION

LAKE

Leesburg

Winter Springs   SEMINOLE

SUMTER

Orlando   Winter Park

Clermont   ORANGE

Kissimmee

St. Cloud

Lakeland

Winter Haven   OSCEOLA

POLK

Bartow

Frostproof

Wauchula   Avon Park

Zolfo Springs

HARDEE

Sebring

HIGHLANDS

Lake Placid

INTRODUCTION

Central Florida Backroads Travel is your mentor to the many attractions and towns in this largest region of the state. Most tourist activity in Central Florida is focused around the locations of the largest theme parks in Florida, and most of them are in Orlando. Walt Disney World, Universal Studios Florida and SeaWorld are all visited at least once by most tourists who visit Florida. In fact, Central Florida is the most popular tourist destination in the world.

Central Florida contains 9 counties: **Marion, Lake, Sumter, Seminole, Orange, Osceola, Polk, Hardee and Highlands.**

These Florida counties sprawl along the high sand ridge that forms the interior of Florida. This ridge was the beach in ancient times, and its surface is made of old rolling sand dunes. This large region starts north of **Ocala** and extends south to the citrus country around **Sebring** and **Lake Placid**. Ocala's rolling hills and pastures are known for producing some of the finest thoroughbred horses in the world.

The center part of this region, around **Orlando** and **Clermont**, was the citrus capital of the state until a big freeze changed things forever. The most recent devastating big chill was in 1982.

Here is a Central Florida Road Map to help you plan your trips.

TOWNS AND CITIES

Central Florida Backroads Travel lists places to stay and eat on many of the individual town pages. The town pages also include a brief history of the town along with my recommended motels, hotels and restaurants. Each town page usually includes a description of at least one bed and breakfast or historic hotel.

The towns and places in Central Florida currently featured on this website are:

Babson Park
Cassadaga
Clermont
Doctor Phillips
Eustis
Fort Meade
Frostproof
Fruitland Park
Haines City
Highland Park
Howey in the Hills
Lakeland
Lake Placid
Lake Wales
Mount Dora
Ocala
Okeechobee
Orlando
Sebring
St Cloud
Tavares
The Villages
Wauchula
Windermere

Winter Garden
Winter Haven
Winter Park

You can't help notice that many towns in this part of Florida have names that start with **Winter**. It can take new residents years to figure out which Winter something is where. Florida travel includes knowing where your "Winters" are. Ones that come to mind are Winter Garden, Winter Haven, Winter Park, Winter Springs and Winter Beach.

The town elders of **Frostproof** just got it over with and came up with the perfect Florida name. The name fascinated tourists when it showed up in early Florida travel brochures.

Babson Park

Babson Park is located on State Road 17 in rural Polk County. A bit more than 1,000 people live in the village nestled on the eastern shore of Crooked Lake among the rolling hills and orange groves. The town is named for **Roger W. Babson**, the founder of Babson College in Massachusetts.

Babson was a well-known businessman and financial expert. He received a degree from Massachusetts Institute of Technology in 1898, and got his LLD from the University of Florida in 1927. That same year, **Grace Knight Babson** and Roger W. Babson founded Webber International University.

Webber was originally established as a women's college, with the exclusive purpose of teaching women about business. It was the first school chartered under the educational and charitable laws of the State of Florida as a non-profit organization.

Male students were first allowed in 1971, and Webber is now a fully accredited coed university of about 400 full time students. It is one of eleven schools recognized by U.S. News & World Report as a "School With a Specialty": Business.

Webber now issues degrees in accounting, computer information systems management, hospitality and tourism management along with many other programs. Babson was the Prohibition Party's candidate for President of the United States in 1940, but he was beat by Franklin D. Roosevelt, Wendell Willkie and Norman Thomas. At least he gave it a try.

Roger Babson lived a long productive life and died in nearby Lake Wales, Florida in 1967 at the age of 91.

Hillcrest Lodge was built in 1917 in the tiny village of Hillcrest Heights on the south edge of Babson Park. It was originally known as the Lakeside Club because of its location on the shore of Crooked Lake.

Many celebrities of the old days stayed at the lodge including **Babe Ruth** and **William Jennings Bryan**. Hillcrest Heights has a population of less than 300 as of 2012.

Hillcrest Lodge was originally built in 1917 in the tiny village of Hillcrest Heights on the south edge of Babson Park. It was originally known as the Lakeside Club because it was built on the shore of Crooked Lake.

BABSON PARK LOCATION MAP

Cassadaga

Cassadaga is about halfway between Orlando and Daytona Beach just off the I-4 corridor. The village was created by **George Colby**, a young man originally from New York. Almost 150 years ago, he attended a séance where he was told that someday he would help create a spiritualist community in the southern United States.

Sure enough, in 1875, Colby was introduced to the wilderness of Central Florida by a spirit guide named **Seneca**. Colby homesteaded in the area, and in 1895 deeded 35 acres to the newly organized **Cassadaga Spiritualist Camp Meeting Association**.

A small spring on Colby's homestead reportedly cured the tuberculosis that he had suffered from for years.

The spiritualist organization still exists, and there are a couple of dozen Victorian area cottages and homes sprinkled across the grounds. Many of them are occupied by mediums, psychics and healers.

The Cassadaga Spiritualist Camp conducts church services on a year round basis. Services are held in the Colby Memorial Temple on Stevens Street. Everyone is welcome to attend the services.

There are 40 Certified Mediums at Cassadaga Spiritualist Camp who give readings, and almost as many Certified Healers who help people tap into their inherent self-healing ability.

The Camp has a bookstore with the area's largest selection of books on traditional Spiritualism and Metaphysics. It also carries a large selection of tapes, CD's, crystals, stones, jewelry, Native American crafts and other unique gift items.

The spiritualist camp made the **National Register of Historic Places** back in 1992; it may be the only time an entire town made the list.

If you don't mind seeing or hearing ghosts now and then, try staying at the lovely **Cassadaga Hotel** right in town. It's a great place to stay while you wander around getting readings and looking at the quaint architecture of the village. And maybe you'll be visited by a friendly ghost.

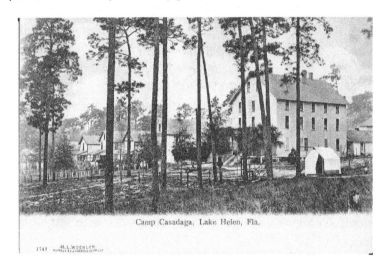

Camp Casadaga, Lake Helen, Fla.

CASSADAGA LOCATION MAP

Clermont

Clermont has something in common with many other small towns and cities in the state. You have to get away from the main highways to discover the real town. The main highways in the Clermont area are **US-27** (a major north-south highway), and **State Road 50** (a major east-west highway that runs from Titusville in the east to Weeki Wachee Springs in the west).

Downtown Clermont is west of the intersection of these two highways. Over the years, major commercial and residential development has taken place around this intersection until the real nature of Clermont is obscured by the hundreds of chain restaurants, service stations and shopping malls.

The town now has about 30,000 people; most of them live in the new developments.

A little searching will take you to historic downtown Clermont. One way to find the original downtown area is to take State Road 50 west from US-27 a few blocks and turn north on 5th Street. You will begin to see historic buildings and know you have stepped back into Old Florida. There is a great city park on the south shore of Lake Minneola, and a historic village that has preserved some of the city's old houses and buildings.

The historic area of Clermont was platted and laid out on the rolling hills between Lake Minneola to the north and Lake Minnehaha to the south. The town was named for the birthplace of one of its founders, **A. F. Wrotnoski**. It's probably fortunate they didn't name the town after him.

In 1922, a developer named **Edward Denslow** organized something called **The Postal Colony Company**. He bought 1,000 acres and planted citrus groves. The groves were owned and tended by the retired post office employees. Clermont was one of the foremost citrus growing towns in America.

One of the most popular tourist attractions in Central Florida was built in Clermont Florida in 1956: the **Florida Citrus Tower**. An elevator took visitors to the top of the tall tower built on a hill northeast of town on US-27. The top of the tower was the highest point in Florida. You could see hundreds of thousands of acres of citrus, and could see all the way to **Orlando**. There was no **Walt Disney World** or other big theme parks in those days. Tourists loved the Citrus Tower.

A serious freeze in the early 1980s destroyed most of the groves in this part of Central Florida. The Orlando metro area was booming, and the land became worth more as residential subdivision property than as groves. Almost nobody replanted their groves, and the result is the populated area you see today

I moved to Florida in 1960, and the old Clermont downtown looks pretty much the same as it did back then, but nicer, with a lot of buildings being restored, trees planted, streets resurfaced. The rest of the area looks like much of the rest of Florida but with lots of rolling hills. A nice place to visit north of town is the **Lakeridge Winery**.

The Clermont Florida area has just about one of every chain restaurant you can imagine. They are all fine, but for a taste of where the locals eat, try the **Downtown Grill**. It's in the heart of downtown Clermont; a quiet place at night, but the Grill attracts the locals and has good food and a full service bar.

CLERMONT FLORIDA LOCATION MAP

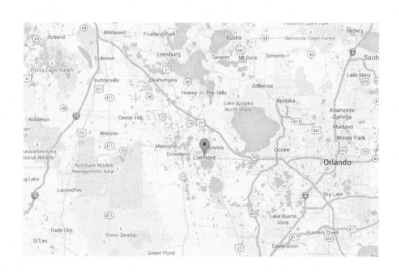

Eustis

Eustis is a town of about 20,000 people about 30 miles northwest of Orlando. Along with **Tavares** and **Mount Dora**, it is one apex of what is known as Florida's **"Golden Triangle"**.

Eustis is on the eastern shore of Lake Eustis, and was first known as Highlands and later as Pendryville. It became known as Lake Eustis after the lake which had been named in 1825 after **Abraham Eustis**, an American general in the Seminole Wars.

Before the railroad showed up in the 1880's, Eustis was a busy port for steamers traveling on Lakes **Harris, Eustis, Dora** and **Griffin.** This chain of lakes had access to the world through the **Ocklawaha River** to the **St Johns River** and the Atlantic ocean.

In 1883 the town dropped the "Lake" part of its name and became simply Eustis.

Citrus became an important crop in the area, but the great freeze of 1894 and 1895 nearly destroyed the industry. Over the years, the fruit trees once again became prominent in the economy of the area.

Eustis has many well preserved older homes and buildings. Its downtown area has been redeveloped and has many interesting shops and restaurants.

An early pioneer's house at the corner of Bay Street and Bates Avenue now houses the Eustis Historical Museum and Preservation Society.

The downtown area along Lake Eustis has been developed into a wonderful park for fishing, picnics and concerts. **Ferran Park** is a great place to watch the Central Florida sunsets.

For some restaurants I like in Eustis, go to the **Mount Dora** page in this guide. I have a list of my favorite restaurants in Eustis, Mount Dora and Tavares.

EUSTIS LOCATION MAP

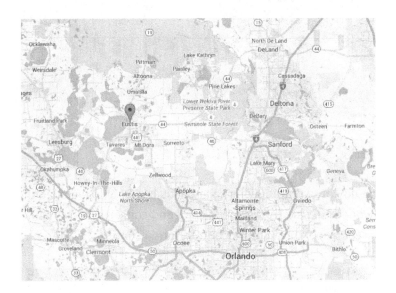

Fort Meade

Fort Meade is a town of about 6,000 people in Polk County southeast of Lakeland. It is the oldest city in Polk County. It is located at the intersection of US-17 and US-98, west of Frostproof. It is on the eastern edge of the phosphate mining region that has created a watery moonscape for many miles west of town.

It was first settled as a U.S. Army fort in 1849 on an old military road from Fort Brooke (Tampa) to Fort Pierce during the Seminole Wars. Although it was originally called Fort Clinch, it was soon renamed after Lt. **George Meade**

George Meade stayed in the Army and later became a prominent general in the U.S. Civil war on the Union Side.

Major General Meade is famous for having defeated **Confederate General Robert E. Lee** at the **Battle of Gettysburg**.

Future Confederate **General Thomas J. "Stonewall" Jackson** was also stationed at the fort in 1851.

The town that grew up around the fort was destroyed by Union forces in 1864 during the Civil War. All of the original buildings were destroyed.

The town was rebuilt after the Civil War, and now Fort Meade has many homes on the **National Register of Historic Places.**

<u>**Christ Episcopal Church**</u> in Fort Meade in an example of Carpenter Gothic architecture. It was built in 1889 and is at 331 E. Broadway. It is on the U.S. National Register of Historic Places. It is an example of the many Carpenter Gothic churches that still stand in Florida.

The **Old Fort Meade School House Museum** is also a fun place to visit. It's in an old building that dates back to 1885. The school house was donated to the Fort Meade Historical society when it was still located on South Lanier Avenue.

Over the years, the building has served not only as a school but as a private residence and a boarding house. It has been a museum since September 2000. The museum is a good place to study photographs of the historic homes in Fort Meade that still exist.

Fort Meade is a quiet place for a Florida history buff to spend a day or a weekend.

RESTAURANTS IN FORT MEADE

Just Ribs, 310 S. Charleston Ave, Fort Meade, FL 33841. 863-286-7625. Best ribs for miles around. They have a devoted following.

FORT MEADE LOCATION MAP

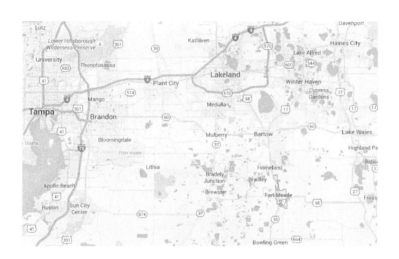

Frostproof

Frostproof is a small town of about 3,000 people on Scenic Highway 17 in Polk County, Florida. It's south of Lake Wales, north of Sebring and east of Winter Haven. Take Highway 630 out of town to the east and you'll go through Yeehaw Junction across lonely prairie on your way to **Vero Beach**. The town is located on an isthmus between **Reedy Lake** and **Lake Clinch**; this favorable situation has a lot to do with the town's moderate winter temperatures.

The town was originally named Keystone City, but people kept getting it confused with Keystone Heights up in North Central Florida. The town fathers, being good developers, came up with the perfect Florida name: Frostproof.

Unfortunately, a couple of years later a severe frost visited the area and destroyed most of the citrus groves in the area. Even so, it is still one of the most "frost proof" areas in the state and the citrus industry still thrives here.

Frostproof is home to two of Florida's legendary agricultural giants: **Ben Hill Griffin, Jr.** (above) and **Lattimore "Latt" Maxcey** (below).

These pioneers controlled most of the ranch and grove land in this part of Florida for years. One of Ben Hill Griffin's descendants is **Katherine Harris**, former Florida Secretary of State during the notorious "**hanging chad**" presidential election debacle of 2000.

Ben Hill Griffin was a University of Florida alumnus and donated enough to his alma mater that the stadium in Gainesville where the Gators play football is known as **Ben Hill Griffin Stadium** at Florida Field. He is also beloved by Gator fans as being one of the boosters that talked **Steve Spurrier** into becoming Gator head football coach.

Although Frostproof sometimes feels like it is in the middle of nowhere, it is actually only about an hour's drive from

Legoland, Walt Disney World, **Universal Studios**, **Sebring** and its raceway and many other central Florida attractions.

A fun thing to do when visiting Frostproof is to walk the **Frostproof Historical Trail**. It can be a self-guided tour that tells you all about the history of the old buildings you will see in town.

The current **Frostproof City Hall** at 111 West 1st Street used to be Frostproof High School in earlier days. It is on the **U. S. National Register of Historic places**.

FROSTPROOF LOCATION MAP

Fruitland Park

Fruitland Park is a small village of about 4,000 people on US-441/US-27 north of Leesburg, Florida. It is on the western shore of **Lake Griffin** in an area known as Dead River. It is near **The Villages Florida** that sprawls west and north of Fruitland Park

The area of the town was originally settled before the American Civil War. The first settler was Calvin Lee, who set out the area's first citrus grove.

Another early settler was a horticulturist named **Major Orlando P. Rooks**. He and his wife built a house on Crystal Lake in 1877. Major Rooks came up with the name Fruitland Park because of all the nurseries and groves that had sprung up in the area. There is an Orlando P. Rooks buried in **Lone Oak Cemetery** in **Leesburg**. The gravestone identifies him as a veteran of Co. D,

Kansas Infantry. Maybe it's the same Mr. Rooks. It would be quite a coincidence if he's a different guy with the same name.

One of the oldest buildings still in use in Fruitland Park is **Holy Trinity Episcopal Church** at 2201 Spring Lake Road. This church is on the U.S. National Register of Historic Places, and is an example of Carpenter Gothic architecture.

FRUITLAND PARK LOCATION MAP

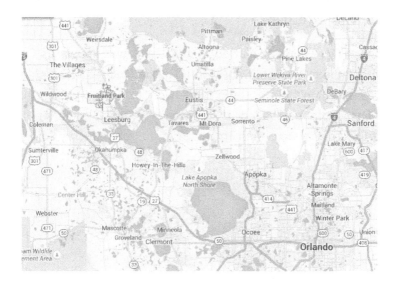

Haines City

Haines City is a town of about 20,000 people in Polk County in Central Florida. It is near the intersection of US-27 and US-17/92. The town is six miles south of Interstate 4, and the entire area around I-4 and US-27 is loosely referred to as Haines City although the town proper is to the south. The northern end of the **Scenic Highway, SR-17**, is in Haines City and follows along the east side of US-27 all the way down to Sebring. It's a drive I recommend you take.

Haines City was first platted in 1885, and was known as Clay Cut. Not long after that, the South Florida Railroad reached the area but didn't put a station in town. Local history says that townspeople persuaded the railroad to build a station by agreeing to rename their town after a railroad official, **Colonel Henry Haines**.

Ten Floors of Modern Comfort — THE POLK — Haines City, Florida

In the early days, and still to some degree, the area was in the middle of some of the most fertile citrus groves in the state. Citrus growing and processing became the main business of Haines City.

One of the major juice companies in the early days was **Donald Duck Citrus**. It was a large employer, and its plant on US-27 in nearby Lake Wales featured a prominent picture of the smart alek duck himself.

Local history says that Disney executives contacted the company in the 1960's and accused them of using the Disney character's name without the proper licenses. The owners of Donald Duck Citrus immediately produced an old yellowed document that proved **Walt and Roy Disney** had given them the rights to the name almost forty years before Disney even thought of moving into Central Florida.

Another major employer was **Suni-Citrus Products Co**. in Haines City, founded by a man named **Emory Cocke.** This company had developed special processes to convert orange peels and pulp into cattle feed. I met Mr. Cocke during my engineering career many years ago, and he was an interesting man. His office ran efficiently even though it looked like it was right out of a 1930 movie with old telephones, typewriters and a general vintage atmosphere of an earlier generation.

In recent years Haines City has seen tremendous population growth because of its easy access to job centers in Tampa, Orlando, Walt Disney World and Universal Studios. Some of this growth has resulted in prosperity as can be seen in the newly opened **Lake Eva Community Center** in the photo above.

New subdivisions have been developed on the edges of the city, especially in the areas near I-4 north of town. These modern developments are in stark contrast with the old **Palm Crest Hotel**, formerly known as the Polk Hotel, in downtown Haines City that has dominated the skyline since the 1920's. Like most small Florida towns, the downtown area is the last to be modernized.

BEST RESTAURANT IN HAINES CITY

Manny's Original Chop House, 35496 Hwy 27, Haines City, FL 33844-3727

HAINES CITY LOCATION MAP

Highland Park

Highland Park is located on Scenic Highway 17 in rural eastern Polk County, Florida, near Babson Park. The population numbers in the low hundreds, but it is an incorporated community, an actual chartered town. The town was founded in 1927, and has always been a recreation focused community. The village is surrounded by an 18-hole golf course designed and built by the well-known firm of **Stiles & Van Kleek in** 1927.

A Lake Wales businessman, **B.K. Bullard**, bought 3,000 acres in 1919 that included what is now Highland Park. Bullard hired **Irwin A. Yarnell** to promote the community and sell lots. Yarnell produced many ads and brochures that are classics of Florida promotion.

Yarnell built a 25 room mansion in 1923 on a hilltop in Highland Park. It is still there today, and presents a great photo opportunity if you can find a place to stand and take the snapshot either from Scenic Highway 17 or the entrance into Highland Park.

"La Casa de Josephina" was a gift to his wife, Josephine, and it overlooks the entire community. Its architecture is typical of the **Florida Boom** era of the 1920's, Moorish looking like a Spanish or Italian palace. The picture above of the Casa was taken in 2007. On a recent visit in January 2012, I observed that the Casa has now been painted a dark brown chocolate color. I don't like it, but different strokes for different folks.

The Village of Highland Park is on the shores of **Lake Easy**. The lake used to be a favorite destination of weekend sea plane buffs who would fly in and have brunch at **Lekarica** resort.

Many of the early Highland Park residents were Quakers. They lived in a dormitory, separated into male and female wings. The dormitory still stands, and is part of the **Lekarica Golf and**

Country Club Resort. The restaurant was not open when I visited on a recent Monday (January 2012), but the original golf course is still played daily by residents and visitors.

The hurricanes in 2004 did a lot of damage to Lekarica, but my recent visit showed that the damage has been repaired. There are plenty of fine vacation cottages on the property and the entire resort is for sale. Step back in time and enjoy this part of Old Florida. It is a magical feeling to wander around Highland Park.

HIGHLAND PARK LOCATION MAP

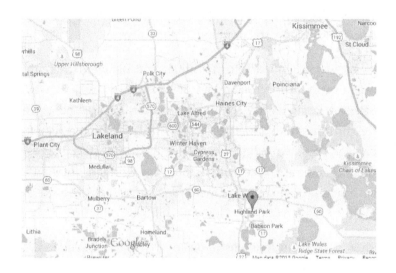

Howey in the Hills

Howey In The Hills is a small rural town of about 1,000 people located in Lake County. It is near **Eustis, Mount Dora** and **Tavares**. This quaint town is on the western shore of **Little Lake Harris** on the Central Florida Harris Chain of Lakes. It's a scenic family-friendly place with many old buildings in the Spanish mission style of architecture. An example is the US Post Office set among beautiful old oak trees.

The town father was **William John Howey**, who built the first citrus juice plant in Florida in 1921. Howey founded Howey In The Hills in 1925, and his mansion along with several other historic buildings is still prominent in the town.

Howey was a visionary for his time, and planned to create a citrus empire in the rolling hills of Lake County with Howey in the Hills Florida as the commercial center. He created a "Tent City" on the shore of Little Lake Harris, and for the first four years of the town's history, he put up prospective buyers in tents. As business picked up, he built the **Floridan Hotel** on the south side of town, and his mansion on the north side. He also built the Floridan Country Club and golf course in 1928.

Other prominent pioneer families in Howey included C. V. Griffin and Dodge Taylor. A small cemetery just south of town on Highway 19 is the final resting place of most of the town's pioneers.

Mr. Griffin converted the Floridan Hotel into the administration for a new school, **Howey Academy**, in 1956, but the school didn't make it and closed in the late 1970's. The building was finally blown up as a prop in a 1994 Hulk Hogan movie. It was sad to see all that history go up in smoke.

In 1964 the Floridan Club property, including the golf course, was purchased by **Nick Beucher** and incorporated into today's **Mission Inn Resort and Club**. This golf and tennis club is a beautiful place and one of the most famous establishments in Lake County and certainly in Howey in the Hills Florida. I attended a corporate retreat at Mission Inn more than 40 years ago. It is even nicer today.

The William Howey mansion still stands on a heavily wooded lot near the entrance to the town on Highway 19. It is difficult to see from the road and is not open to the public. It is not occupied as of 2015 and is slowly deteriorating in the hot Florida sun.

Stop by **Boondocks** on Little Lake Harris on the south side of town and enjoy a cold beer and a good hot meal. Just north and west of Howey is the **Yalaha Bakery**, a real operating bakery that is fun to visit and has sandwiches, coffee, wine, beer and entertainment in addition to their famous bread products.

HOWEY IN THE HILLS LOCATION MAP

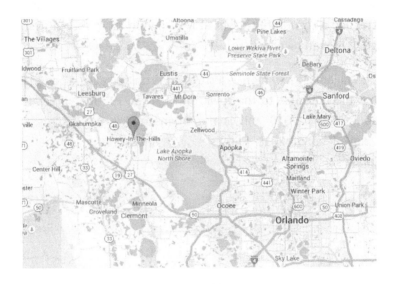

Lakeland

Lakeland is a city of about 90,000 people in Polk County. It is in the center of a metro area that has more than 500,000 people. Lakeland is in the I-4 corridor between Orlando and Tampa. It is one of the prettiest of all Florida towns. It is liberally dotted with beautiful small lakes and has a large swan population that lives and prospers among the lakes.

Swan sculptures are placed all over town and seem to be the mascot of choice. Lake Morton and Lake Mirror are in the downtown area, and are home to hundreds of swans.

Lakeland Florida was first settled in the years after the Civil War, and began to grow quickly once the railroads came to town in 1884.

The town was founded by Abraham Munn, who purchased 80 acres in what is now downtown Lakeland.

The Florida land boom of the 1920's saw many major buildings go up in downtown Lakeland. Many of these are still standing and are on the National Register of Historic Places, including the Terrace Hotel and New Florida Hotel, now known as Regency Towers.

Lakeland also has numerous historic districts with buildings that go back the 1920's, 30's and 40's. Many parks are in these neighborhoods, including several of them around Lake Mirror.

Frank Lloyd Wright came to town in 1938 and spent the next 20 years working on designs for various buildings on the **Florida Southern** campus. He designed 18 buildings, and 9 of them were built and are still standing.

All of the buildings are in daily use as offices and classrooms.

Florida Southern has the largest collection of Frank Lloyd Wright buildings in the world. It was recently announced that the school is going to build one of Wright's famous Usonian homes on campus.

Tours are available to visit the Wright designed buildings and learn about their history. Contact the Florida Southern College Visitor center at 863-680-4597 for more information.

For many years, up until the 1970's, Lakeland's nickname was the **"All American City"**. It was considered a bellwether for all of the United States. It was believed that if a concept worked in Lakeland, it was likely to succeed elsewhere.

In 1968, I had lunch at the first **Red Lobster** to ever open in this country on the first week it opened. It was on Lake Ellenor Drive on Lake Parker. My fried flounder platter cost $ 1.69. The same meal today is about 8 times as much.

Lakeland is also the home of **Publix,** Florida's premier grocery chain. Its founder, **George Jenkins**, died some years ago but is fondly referred to by Publix employees as "Mr. George".

Former US Senator and Florida Governor, the late **Lawton Chiles**, was also a native of Lakeland.

Today's Lakeland Florida is a great place to visit, shop, dine and just enjoy the parks and swans.

LAKELAND RESTAURANTS

Harry's Seafood Bar and Grille, 101 N. Kentucky Avenue, Lakeland, FL. 863-686-2228. Great atmosphere, wonderful food and drinks in the heart of downtown Lakeland.

LAKELAND HOTELS

Terrace Hotel,
329 East Main Street
Lakeland, Florida 33801
Tel: 863-688-0800

This hotel was built in 1924 and was restored to luxury hotel status in 1998. It has 73 guest rooms and 15 suites. This great place in downtown Lakeland is on the **National Register of Historic Places**.

LAKELAND LOCATION MAP

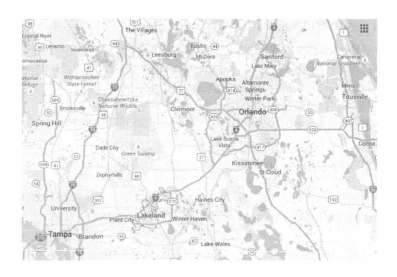

Lake Placid

Lake Placid is in Highlands County. Its population is about 2,000. Its nearest big neighbor is Sebring a short distance north through several miles of rolling hills among fragrant orange groves along US-27. The town is a mecca for mural lovers, with more than 40 murals painted on buildings throughout the town. These murals transform what was a typical little Florida town into an outdoor art gallery.

The town was originally called Lake Stearns and was founded in 1925. **Dr. Melvil Dewey**, the inventor of the **Dewey Decimal System**, bought a lot of acreage in the area. He was the founder of the **Lake Placid Club** in New York, and convinced the town and state to go along with changing the name of Lake Stearns to Lake Placid.

Lake Placid is also famous for producing 98 percent of the world's caladium bulbs. To celebrate this distinction, the town holds an **Annual Caladium Festival**. This festival has tons of bulbs and plants for sale, along with dozens of arts and craft booths and a lot of other exhibits.

Lake Placid is a good place to start a day trip around the lakes in the area, including Lake Placid and **Lake June-In-Winter.**

Henscratch Farms Winery is west of Lake Placid and is worth a visit. There are also neat little Mom and Pop motels along the shore of Lake June-In-Winter making it a nice vacation destination.

An nice day trip is to go south from Lake Placid along SR-17, also known locally as **Old State Road 8**. It will take you down to the ghost towns of Venus and Old Venus about 12 miles south through rolling grove country. A relic of bygone days is the **Lake Placid Tower**. It is now closed down to the public.

LAKE PLACID LOCATION MAP

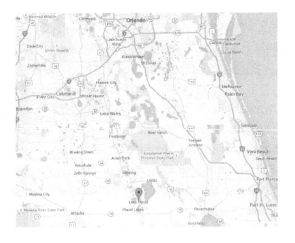

Lake Wales

Lake Wales is a town of about 11,000 people in Polk County. The town lies next to the intersection of US-27 and SR-60, two of Florida's major highways in the days before interstates. It is located west of Lake Kissimmee and east of Tampa. Downtown Lake Wales is on **Scenic Highway State Road 17.** This scenic highway takes you north to **Haines City** through hundreds of thousands of acres of citrus groves.

If you take it south you will go through even more groves on your way to **Babson Park, Frostproof, Avon Park** and **Sebring**.

The land that now includes Lake Wales was surveyed by **Sidney Irving Wailes** in 1879. He changed the name of a nearby lake, Watts Lake, to **Lake Wailes**.

The town of Lake Wales was established next to this lake in 1911-12 by the Lake Wales Land Company. The spelling **Wales**

was used for the city, although the lake is still generally spelled Lake Wailes....if you can remember to do it.

In 1925 the Atlantic Coast Line Railroad built a new line from Haines City through Lake Wales on the way to Everglades City way down south near Naples. A depot was opened in the downtown area.

At one time Lake Wales was best known for the **Mountain Lake Club**, a private community founded in 1915, with a top-ranked golf course designed in 1916 by Seth Raynor. Mountain Lake has a fascinating history and is part of Florida lore not always found in the history books.

The community was founded in 1915 by **Frederick S. Ruth** of Baltimore. He bought 3,500 acres in the hilly, fertile land, which is among the highest in the state of Florida.

Ruth hired **Frederick Law Olmsted, Jr.** to lay out 600 acres of the property for the residences and brought in Seth Raynor to design the golf course. Olmsted had designed **Central Park** in New York and **Biltmore Estates** in Asheville, North Carolina, so he was no slouch.

Mountain Lake has only 125 residences, few of them within sight of the golf course, so the gently rolling land is open and space is abundant within the very private grounds. The Mountain Lake Historic District is on the **National Register of Historic Places**.

In the mid-1920s **Edward W. Bok**, the publisher of **The Saturday Evening Post** and **The Ladies Home Journal**, owned a home at Mountain Lake. He had come to America from Holland and became very successful in his career. He wanted to give something back to his new country, so he acquired over 100 acres of the highest land in the Lake Wales area and created **Historic Bok Sanctuary**.

The **"Singing Tower"** is one of the world's most renowned carillons, and outdoor concerts and other events are scheduled on a regular basis. Bok Sanctuary also hosts an international festival of carillonneurs each year.

Lake Wales Florida is still a fascinating city, with the old 1920's vintage hotel still dominating the downtown skyline.

LAKE WALES LOCATION MAP

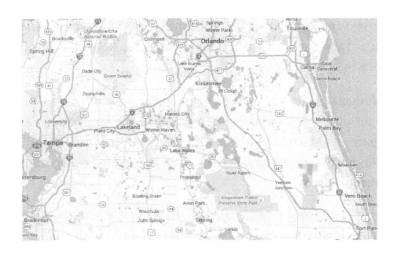

Mount Dora

Mount Dora Is a beautiful lakefront town in the wooded hills northwest of Orlando in Lake County. The population is about 12,000. Mount Dora has many antique shops in the downtown area, and a huge antique center called **Renninger's** on the outskirts of town. Downtown Mount Dora overlooks beautiful Lake Dora on the Harris Chain of Lakes.

One of the most unusual attractions for this lakefront Central Florida town is its lighthouse. It is one of only three freshwater lighthouses in Florida. The citizens of Mount Dora got together and financed it. It was built in 1988 and is owned and operated by the City of Mount Dora. The lighthouse is a favorite photo backdrop for residents and tourists alike, and is a featured attraction on the local Segway tour.

The history of Mount Dora began in 1874 when the area was settled by David Simpson, his wife and 2 children. In 1880, Ross Tremain became the first postmaster, and the community was named "**Royellou**" after his three children, Roy, Ella and Louis. Some of his descendants are still prominent in the town.

In 1883, The Alexander House opened, a 2 story hotel with 10 rooms, and the community was renamed **"Mount Dora"**. It was named after Lake Dora, which had been named by surveyors in 1846 for **Dora Ann Drawdy**, an early settler. Dora is memorialized today in the name of Dora Drawdy Way, a cute little gentrified downtown alley. The history of Mount Dora is kept alive throughout the town in the names of streets and buildings.

THINGS TO DO IN MOUNT DORA

Mount Dora always seems to have something interesting going on. The town hosts an annual art festival, craft fair, plant and garden show and many other special events including classic car shows. Here are some recurring events that will give you a reason to visit Mount Dora several times a year.

JANUARY

Renninger's Antique Extravaganza. The extravaganzas are held on the third weekends of January, February and November at Renningers Twin Markets of US-441 in Mount Dora, Florida. Each one of them is a large gathering of more than 1500 antique dealers hauling in their goods from all over the country. For more information, call 352-383-8393.

FEBRUARY

Annual Arts Festival is held on the first Weekend in February. This nationally recognized fine arts festival attracts almost 300 artists from all over the country and other nations. The art is displayed on the streets of downtown Mount Dora and attracts thousands of art lovers. For more information call the Mount Dora Center for the Arts. 352-383-0880.

Annual Mount Dora Music Festival, held on the third weekend in February. Presentation of artistic music including classical, big band and jazz. For more information call 352-385-1010. The music is often presented at the spacious Mount Dora Community Center. More information is available at the website http://mountdoramusicfest.com/.

MARCH

Mount Dora Annual Spring Show, held on the fourth weekend of March. 200 vendors display their crafts on the streets of downtown Mount Dora, Florida. For more information call Mount Dora Village Merchants & Business Association, 352-735-1191.

APRIL

Festival of Reading, held on the first weekend of April. Writer's contests, meet your favorite authors and various readings. Held at the W.T. Bland Public Library. For more information call 352-735-7180.

Annual Sail Boat Regatta, held on the first weekend of April. The oldest regatta in Florida is fun for the entire family and takes place on Lake Dora near the **Mount Dora Yacht Club**. For more information call 352-383-3188.

MAY

Annual Taste in Mount Dora, held on Third Sunday in May. A delicious evening of fantastic food prepared by the finest restaurants in the Golden Triangle Area of Mount Dora, Tavares and Eustis held at Lake Receptions between 5-8PM. Contact Mount Dora Chamber of Commerce, 352-383-2165.

JULY

July 4th Independence Day Celebration. A great celebration of our Independence Day of the United States of America with a parade, food and live music. It starts with a downtown parade at 10am, then other activities from 5-9pm at Gilbert Park with fireworks about 9pm. For more information please call 352-383-2165.

OCTOBER

Annual Bicycle Festival, second weekend in October. This major event draws more than 1,000 cyclists. It is Florida's oldest and largest bicycling event, with rides of varying lengths and levels of skill and difficulty. Cyclists of all ages come and see why Lake County is recognized as one of the best places in the world to ride according to the March 1998 edition of Bicycling Magazine. For more information call 352-383-2165.

Annual Craft Fair, fourth weekend in October. This nationally ranked juried event continues to attract over 250,000 visitors and over 350 of the best craftspeople in the country. It is held on the streets of downtown Mount Dora. For more information call 352-735-1191

NOVEMBER

Annual Mount Dora Plant & Garden Fair, held the first weekend in November. Admission is free. Central Florida plant growers display more than 12,000 plants at Simpson's Cove on the downtown Mount Dora waterfront. There are orchid displays and exhibits of native Florida plants, perennials, herbs, roses, camellias, begonias and rare tropical plants. Garden antiques and unique containers are also on display. For more information call 352-729-2170

Lake and Hills Garden Club Annual Garden Tour, first weekend in November. The club will lead tours of several distinctive gardens. Club members will be on hand to describe each garden and answer questions. Cost is $12 prior to the event and $15 day of event. Tours begin at the **Country Club of Mount Dora** on Highland Avenue (Old U.S. Highway 441). For more information go to lakesandhillsgardenclub.com.

Annual Light Up Mount Dora, is held the Saturday after Thanksgiving. There is a lighting ceremony between 5 and 9pm each year in downtown Mount Dora at Donnelly Park, with the lights actually being turned on at 630pm. Close to 2 million sparkling lights are illuminated and Santa Claus makes a visit. This event draws people from all over Lake County, Orlando and the surrounding area. For more information call 352-383-2165

DECEMBER

Christmas Walk, a holiday street party on the second Friday after Thanksgiving. Sometimes this is in November, sometimes in December, with music, Santa and shopping in downtown Mount Dora between 6pm-9pm. For more information call 352-383-2165.

Annual Christmas Parade, first Saturday of December, held at 1pm on the streets of downtown Mount Dora. For more information call 352-735-9629.

Lighted Boat Parade, first Saturday of December, held each year on the Mount Dora waterfront near the Mount Dora Yacht Club. For more information call 352-735-9629.

The **Donnelly House** is on Donnelly Street, the main drag of Mount Dora. It was built by an early mayor and is on the National Register of Historic Places. It is used today as a Masonic Lodge.

The vintage postcard below shows **Donnelly Street** looking north. If you stand on the corner of 4th Avenue and Donnelly today you will recognize most of the features on this card. One sad difference is that the big tree on the corner is not longer there.

The tall white building on the left is today's Renaissance Building, home to many shops and restaurants, but one a thriving hotel in the downtown district.

MOUNT DORA HOTELS

Adora Inn, 610 N. Tremain St., Mount Dora, Florida 32757. Enjoy a gourmet breakfast in the dining room or peaceful front porch, relax in your beautifully appointed guest room or plan you next special event at Adora Inn. Located in the heart of the historical district in charming Mount Dora, Adora Inn is walking distance to the town's restaurants, shops, festivals, parks and only a short thirty minute drive to the Orlando theme parks. Adora Inn is a comfortable retreat for the sophisticated traveler. It is rated 3 diamonds by AAA, and was picked No. 1 for romantic weekend get-a-way by a Central Florida magazine.

Grandview Bed & Breakfast. 442 East 3rd Avenue, Mount Dora, FL 32757. Tel: 352-383-4440.This lovely inn is just two blocks from downtown Mount Dora. This was originally the William Watt house, built in the early 1900's, and has been restored with rooms having private baths, queen beds, central air conditioning and heat. Full breakfast is served.

Lakeside Inn. 100 North Alexander Street, Mount Dora, Florida 32757. Tel: 352-383-4101. The Inn is the centerpiece of downtown Mount Dora with cozy rooms and good dining right on the shores of Lake Dora. On the National Register of Historic Places, Lakeside Inn was established in 1883. In 2010 a new owner took over who is renovating many of the hotel rooms. The Beauclair Room is the hotel's main dining room, open to the public, and right next door is Tremain's Lounge, a favorite hangout for locals. On cool evenings a fireplace crackles away in the corner of Tremain's. The front porch of the hotel is a great place to sit and rock and people watch and gaze out over beautiful Lake Dora.

Mount Dora Historic Inn. 221 East 4th Avenue, Mount Dora, Florida 32757. Tel: 352-735-1212. This historic inn is just a block or two from downtown Mount Dora on a shady tree lined street. The inn was built in the 1880's and has been lovingly restored with beautifully appointed rooms with private baths.

MOUNT DORA RESTAURANTS

The next section in this book lists my favorite restaurants in Mount Dora, Eustis and Tavares. I've personally tried and enjoyed these places. If it isn't on my list, I either didn't try it or didn't enjoy it.

MOUNT DORA LOCATION MAP

Mount Dora Restaurants

The Mount Dora restaurants on this page only include those that I've tried and liked. If it's not on the list, either I didn't try it, didn't like it or have forgotten to write it up.

Mount Dora is one of the three towns that make up Central Florida's "Golden Triangle". Mount Dora restaurants on this page also include those in the other two triangle towns: **Eustis** and **Tavares**.

The list might be a bit Mount Dora centric because that's where I live.

RECOMMENDED RESTAURANTS

Buzzard Beach Bar and Grill. 2050 W Burleigh Blvd, Tavares, FL 32778. This little place is on the south shore of Lake Eustis on US-441 just west of Tavares. Dining on the dock, great place for sunsets, nice screened dining room with plenty of tables and weekend entertainment. Good place by boat or car or bike. Great hamburgers and French fries. Beer, wine and full liquor bar.

Cafe Gianni. 425 North Alexander Street, Mount Dora, FL 32757. This little restaurant had a nice following in Eustis and moved the entire operation to Mount Dora in 2014. It has an upscale Italian menu in a two story building in downtown Mount Dora. Dining upstairs or down; wine and beer. Chicken, pork, beef and seafood. Homemade pasta.

Chili's Bar & Grill. 17419 Us Hwy 441, Mount Dora, FL 32757. Tel: 352-589-4002. Yep, this is the big national chain and I like it a lot. Good chili, fajitas, hamburgers, wide variety of menu items. Full liquor bar and great margaritas. One of the best of the chain Mount Dora restaurants.

Cody's on 4th. 111 East 4th Avenue, Mount Dora, FL 32757. Tel: 352-735-8426. Nice little cafe decorated with old scenes of historic Mount Dora. They have a variety of coffee, homemade pastries, fresh salads, sandwiches, beer and wine.

Copacabana Cuban Cafe. 320 Dora Drawdy Way, Mount Dora Florida 32757. Tel: 352-385-9000. This is a great place to eat. Simple yet comfortable decor and interior. Owner Alberto and his staff are very attentive and agreeable. Food is great and served promptly. I recently had picadillo - a lightly spiced ground beef dish - served with plantains and yellow rice. As an appetizer, I had sopa de pollo - chicken soup- with lots of noodles, potatoes, carrots, and chicken. It was only $4.95 and could have been a meal unto itself. My picadillo was just right. This is a good place to eat and to discover that Mount Dora restaurants include a good Cuban place.

Fiesta Grande Mexican Grill. 421-B Baker Street, Mount Dora Florida 32757. Tel: 352-385-3540. This is a large, bright and cheerful downtown eatery that has a full liquor bar and a wide range of Mexican dishes. Very good food and colorful atmosphere. There are other Mount Dora restaurants that feature Mexican food, but this is my favorite.

Golden Corral Buffet & Restaurant. 15810 Us Highway 441, Eustis, FL 32726. Tel: 352-589-1831. This restaurant features a big buffet that is sure to have something on it you will like. The salad bar is great with plenty of lettuce, carrots, green peppers, black olives, croutons, cole slaw and a host of other goodies like garbanzos and cheeses. The hot meal bar is loaded with a lot of fried delights like fish, chicken, okra and other southern staples like green beans and carrots. They also have an excellent rotisserie chicken. They also have great desserts. Prices reasonable, service great.

Highland Street Cafe. 185 South Highland Street, Mount Dora Florida 32757. Tel: 352-383-1446. This is one of the Mount Dora restaurants favored by locals, especially as a breakfast place, although they also have a regular American lunch menu. It is similar to a diner in menu and layout. Breakfast is available all day long. Service is great and food is good, especially breakfast.

Jeremiah's. 947 East 5th Avenue, Mount Dora Florida 32757. Tel: 352-383-7444. This corner restaurant is a good place for dinner. They have just about everything, and their fajitas are better than any of the chain restaurants on the outskirts of town. Jeremiah's has a full liquor bar, and outside dining is available too.

Kiku Japanese Steakhouse. 15211 US Highway 441, Eustis, FL 32726. 352-483-8288. This large and roomy restaurant is in the Publix shopping center at David Walker Boulevard. It features great hibachi, cooked at your table while you watch in amazement. It is one of two Mount Dora restaurants that feature hibachi cooking. Full liquor bar, reasonable prices.

Lampu Japanese Steakhouse. US Highway 441 # 2, Mount Dora Florida 32757. Tel: 352-383-6119. This large restaurant is at the north end of Donnelly Street where it meets US Highway 441 on the north side of town. Lampu features great hibachi, cooked at your table in entertaining fashion. It is one of two Mount Dora restaurants that feature hibachi cooking. Full liquor bar, reasonable prices.

Maggie's Attic. 237 West 4th Avenue, Mount Dora, FL 32757. Tel: 352-383-5451. I have decided that **wine and beer are food** for purposes of listing Mount Dora restaurants. I stopped by here recently for one of their "Wine Down Wednesday" events. Probably a hundred jovial people were enjoying beer, wine and music. There was a table set up with snacks, although this is more of a wine, beer and gift shop than a restaurant.

Magical Meat Boutique. 112 W. 4th Avenue Mount Dora, FL 32757. Tel: 352-729-6911. This small place features English dishes and an excellent selection of beer on tap. It calls itself a "carvery restaurant" and is patterned after a family owned butcher shop of the same name in London. Some of the dishes include fish and chips, bangers and mash, Scotch eggs and breakfast any time. I love their 7 item breakfast where you get to choose the items. Phil Barnard and wife Kate are almost always on the premises and will make you feel welcome.

Mr. Cebiche & Tapas, 411 N. Donnelly St., Mount Dora, FL 32757. Tel: 352-735-8106. This is a restaurant specializing in Peruvian food. Located in the second floor of the Renaissance Building in downtown Mount Dora. Great cebiche (or ceviche if you prefer). Other great seafood and meat offerings.

Mount Dora Brewing Company. 405 South Highland St. Mount Dora Florida 32757. Quaint little place with great homemade beer and good wine selection. Try their sliders; you will love them. The rambling building is made up of several unique spaces for drinking and dining-- the Tap Room, Beer Garden, and Dining Room. Lunch is served 7 days a week, and a traditional breakfast on Saturdays and Sundays. Open in the evenings Friday through Monday. Live music is featured in the Tap Room every Friday and Saturday night, and there's an open jam session on Sundays around 5pm.

Norm's Palette, 303 N. Baker Street, Suite 100, Mount Dora, Florida 32757. Tel: 352-729-6196. Norm Rinne is an artist, and his neat little bistro shows it. Light menu, including tapas, shrimp, hummus and cheese platters, small pizzas, sandwiches and other specials. Good selection of beer and wine served among all kinds of art. A pleasant atmosphere, with music now and then. Room for dancing. Nice little cozy bar and private rooms. Outside dining.

Oakwood Smokehouse & Grill. 2911 David Walker Blvd, Eustis, Florida 32726. The inside of this barbecue place reminds you of a gentlemen's hunting club with stuffed deer, boar, bobcats, gator heads and mounted fish. Very good ribs, grilled and barbecued chicken, good slaw and vegetable side dishes. Beer and wine. A pleasant place with reasonably priced good food.

One Flight Up. 440 North Donnelly Street, Mount Dora Florida 32757. Tel: 407-758-9818. This charming little restaurant has outside balcony dining and the best view of downtown of all Mount Dora restaurants. The coffee, soups, salads, wraps and other light fare are among the best in Central Florida. I recommend their Chicken Tuscany soup; a bowl makes a hearty meal. One Flight Up also has several small intimate rooms with comfortable couches and chairs for group gatherings. A good selection of wine and beer will complement your meal.

Pisces Rising. 239 W 4th Ave, Mt Dora FL 32757. Tel: 352-385-2669. I was in Mount Dora the other day looking for a nice place to watch the sunset over Lake Dora. I found myself at the bar on the deck of Pisces Rising. Wonderful bartenders, congenial customers and a great view of the sunset over Lake Dora. I had a scotch and water for $2.25 and a pound of peel and eat shrimp for $10.00. I discovered later that the food inside the restaurant is also great, but pricier than the bar menu. Some locals call this favorite place "Prices Rising", but it is among the most popular of Mount Dora restaurants. The price must be right!

PizzAmore. 722 E 5th Ave, Mt Dora, FL 32757. Tel: 352-383-0092. This restaurant with the catchy name is one of the most popular Mount Dora restaurants. In a nicely restored old home, it is close to downtown, with great salads, pizzas, wine and beer. Order your pizza the way you like: cheesy or not, thin or not, crispy or not. They will make it your way.

Rocking Café. 622 North Donnelly St., Mount Dora, Florida 32757. Tel: 352-720-5951. This new place opened in late 2016 and is already a favorite with locals. Good salads, gyros, hamburgers and more. Wine and beer, inside and outside dining.

Side Lines Sports Eatery. 315 North Highland Street, Mount Dora, FL 32757. Tel: 352-735-7433. This is a typical sports bar with a few TV screens and a good menu standard fare like hamburgers, fries and pizzas. They will make your pizza the way you like it. A local hangout for good old boys and their wives and families. Good service, plenty of parking.

Sol De Mexico. 125 N. Bay Street, Eustis, Florida. Tel: 352-357-0259. Nice Mexican restaurant in the heart of revitalized downtown Eustis. Great standards like tacos, burritos and fajitas. Pleasant decor, sit down dining, good service. Parking lot on east side of restaurant.

Takis Pizza House II, 1600 S Bay St Eustis, FL 32726. Tel: 352-357-0022. As the name implies, Takis has great pizza. I value their Greek dishes, including a great gyro plate, wonderful Greek salads, and my all-time favorite: grape leaves stuffed with ground beef and rice. Good selection of beer and wine.

Thai Jasmine & Sushi House. 1010 E Alfred St., Tavares, Florida 32778, Tel: 352-742-0956. Small place in a strip shopping center but big flavor in sushi and Thai favorites. Friendly staff, wine and beer while you wait.

The Frog and Monkey Restaurant & Pub. 411 North Donnelly St, Mount Dora, FL 32757. Tel: 352-383-1936. This basement bar and eatery is entered either from Donnelly Street or Dora Drawdy Way. It is in the Renaissance Building, the tallest structure in downtown Mt Dora. It is themed as an English Pub. It serves great food, beer and wine. A very good cottage pie, great burgers and soups.

The Goblin Market. 330 Dora Drawdy Way, Mt Dora FL 32757. Tel: 352-735-0059. This fine restaurant is entered from a charming alley between Donnelly and Alexander in the heart of downtown Mount Dora. The atmosphere is charming, reminiscent of a private club with book lined walls and comfortable lighting. The food and service are as good as any place in Florida. Try the upstairs bar for great service. This is the top of "must visit" Mount Dora restaurants.

The Great Pizza Company. 23 E. Magnolia Ave., Eustis, Florida 32726. Located in the historic downtown area of Eustis, this small place with high ceilings and family ambience has about 40 seats and serves fantastic New York style thin crust pizza and good salads. Owner Sandy Johnson says the pizza is so good because they use dough made with New York water. My pizza crust was nice and thin and crispy, just the way I like it.

The Windsor Rose Tea Room & Restaurant. 142 West 4th Ave., Mount Dora, Florida 32757. Tel: 352-735-2551. This comfortable little restaurant is decorated with photos and memorabilia of the British Royal Family. Although they serve high tea in the traditional manner, they also have more conventional lunches like traditional hearty British favorites of pot pies and Cornish pasties, to a selection of tea sandwiches, scones and pastries for Afternoon Tea. Open 7 days a week from 11:00 am to 4:30 pm.

Village Coffee Pot. 425 North Donnelly St, Mt Dora FL. Tel: 352-383-3334. This is the spot to go for great coffee, ice cream, gelato, soup and sandwiches. Not only that, owner **Akhtar** and his strong right hand woman, **Carol**, know what's going on around town and will share the latest information. This small spot in the heart of downtown has become the "nerve central" of downtown Mount Dora. A good place to swap stories and meet old and new friends.

Whales Tale Fish House. 2720 Old US HWY 441, Mount Dora, Florida 32757. Tel: 352-385-1500. Locals have voted it among the top Mount Dora restaurants. It is a bright clean spotless gem and serves great seafood. Crab soup, chowder, clam strips, shrimp, fish and chips. Catfish, haddock, sometimes even grouper, broiled in lemon butter or lightly breaded and fried in canola oil. Beer and wine are available. Service is prompt, excellent and with a smile. Family owned by Pat and Bonnie Duffy. Next door to Mount Dora Pizza.

Ocala

Ocala is a bustling Central Florida town south of **Gainesville** and north of **The Villages** Florida. Its population is about 55,000 people but it's in the middle of a metro area of about 350,000. The town takes its name from **Ocal**i, a major center of the **Timucua Indians** in the 1600's. The name in the Indian language means **"big hammock"**.

Not long after Florida became a territory in 1821, the U.S. Army built **Fort King** near what is now Ocala. The fort was one of many in Florida to protect white settlers from the Seminole Indians. Modern day Ocala, established in 1846, grew up around Fort King.

The railroad came through Ocala in 1881, and the town began to boom. The boom was slowed down, however, when most of downtown Ocala burned down in 1883. Most of the downtown buildings were replaced with brick buildings and Ocala became known by many in the state as **"The Brick City"**.

Citrus was the biggest industry in the area until the freezes of 1894 and 1895 wiped out nearly all of the groves.

As Florida began to grow in the years after World War Two, Ocala became a well-known tourist destination. Some of the local attractions included Silver Springs, Wild Waters Water Park and Six Gun Territory. Silver Springs is now owned by the State and is Silver Springs State Park.

These days the rolling hills around Ocala are known as prime territory for raising thoroughbred horses.

Carl Rose developed the first farm for thoroughbred horses, **Rosemere Farm**, during World War Two on acreage along State Road 200. Rose noted during earlier visits that the limestone that underlies much of the area helps provide nutrients that help build strong and fast horses.

Gornil, one of Rosemere's first horses, won a race at **Miami Tropical Park**. It was the first thoroughbred raised in Florida to win a major race. Soon after this, other thoroughbred operations began to show up in Florida.

Rosemere Farm is now gone, paved over by **Paddock Mall** and **Central Florida College**.

Ocala is now internationally famous for its thoroughbreds. in 1956 Needles became the first Florida raised horse to win the Kentucky Derby. Affirmed won the Triple Crown in 1978.

These successes have helped the area around Ocala become one of the biggest thoroughbred centers in the world. There are almost 1000 thoroughbred farms and another few hundred horse farms devoted to other breeds.

Ocala Florida and Marion County have been among the fastest growing places in the United States since the 1970's. A lot of the growth is due to the attraction of the area as a good place to retire. The Villages Florida and the developments along State Road 200 are now home to thousands of retirees.

Ocala has done an excellent job preserving historic buildings and residences in its downtown area. Several structures are on the National Register of Historic Places. Many of the beautiful old Victorian homes are in the neighborhoods along East Fort King Street.

Equestrian statues are a focal point of the downtown area. You will see dozens of them as you ride around the area, all of them beautiful and eye catching.

OCALA RESTAURANTS

Amrit Palace Indian Restaurant, 3415 SW College Rd, Ocala, FL 34474. 352-873-8500. I love Indian food and this place has some of the best in Central Florida.

OCALA HOTELS

Hampton Inn and Suites, 3601 SW 38th Ave, Ocala, FL 34474.

855-271-3622.

OCALA LOCATION MAP

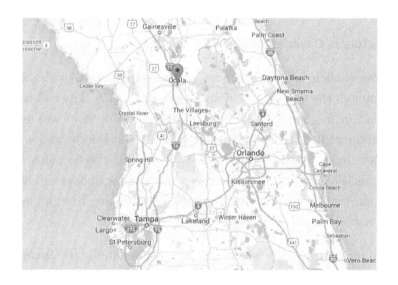

Okeechobee

Okeechobee is the county seat of Okeechobee County, the immediate area surrounding **Lake Okeechobee**. Although it is East Central Florida as described in our series of travel guides, it seems more at home in the vast cattle and citrus lands of Central Florida.

About 6,000 people live in Okeechobee. Some Floridians also refer to the town as **"Okeechobee City"**. It is located at the intersections of State Road 70, US-441, US-98 and County Road 710, a couple of miles north of Lake Okeechobee.

History of Okeechobee Florida

Okeechobee became the seat of government in Okeechobee County. The County courthouse was built in 1926. City Hall was built in the same year. In its early years the town was the center of the cattle industry in south Central Florida, and was also the cornerstone of Florida's freshwater fishing industry, especially catfish and perch. Those same industries are important today, as well as tourism. People come from all over the world to enjoy fishing in Lake Okeechobee.

An important battle was fought in this area during the **Second Seminole War**. The **Battle of Lake Okeechobee** was fought between 800 troops under the command of **Colonel Zachary Taylor**, and about half that many Seminole warriors led by **Billy Bowlegs**, **Abiaca** and **Alligator** on Christmas Day, 1837.

Both the Seminoles and Americans claimed victory, but Colonel Taylor was promoted to Brigadier General after the battle. His nickname of **"Old Rough and Ready"** was invented after this battle, and he went on to become the **12th President of the United States**.

The downtown area of Okeechobee is a wide grassy boulevard with some military monuments and artifacts and shady places to sit and enjoy the view. There are plenty of shops and restaurants in town, and a couple of very nice murals and historic buildings.

Fishing is a main industry in the town, with catfish, bass and speckled perch being the main catches. It is also an agricultural center for Okeechobee Country. The **Speckled Perch Festival** is held annually in March in honor of the famous Lake Okeechobee fish.

Okeechobee and other towns around Lake Okeechobee were devastated by the **1928 Okeechobee Hurricane**. This hurricane was the first recorded Category 5 hurricane in the Atlantic, and is still one of the deadliest hurricanes ever to strike the United States.

Many people were killed by the flooding that followed this hurricane. The low areas around the lake were enclosed within a new dike, named the Herbert Hoover Dike after the President of the United States at that time.

Other towns around Lake Okeechobee include **Buckhead Ridge, Lakeport, Taylor Creek, Port Mayaca, Canal Point, Pahokee, South Bay, Belle Glade, Clewiston,Moore Haven** and a few smaller places.

The eastern, southern and northern shores of Lake Okeechobee are home to many RV parks and fish camps where serious fishermen spend their days casting a line into the big waters.

Okeechobee has some nice murals on various buildings downtown and some interesting displays like this old tractor in front of a bank.

OKEECHOBEE LOCATION MAP

Orlando

Orlando is strategically located in the center of Florida. When Walt Disney was looking at places in the 1960's for his new theme park, he observed that Orlando is in the center of the state and served by major highways. This is still true all these years later, even more so. The city is at the intersection of **I-4** and the **Florida Turnpike**, and is surrounded by one of the country's greatest toll systems. Other major roads that go through town are **US-17, US-92, SR-50** and **US-441**.

It has saddened me for years that most of the millions of tourists who visit central Florida's theme parks each year have never seen the real Orlando. Walt Disney World, for example, is almost 20 miles west of downtown Orlando Florida. International Drive, Lake Buena Vista, Osceola County and the area around the theme parks have expanded to serve the tourists, but they are not the real Orlando.

Orlando Florida History

Orlando's modern history dates back to 1838 and the Second Seminole War. The U.S. Army built Fort Gatlin southeast of present day downtown Orlando to protect settlers from the Indians. By 1840, a small settlement known as Jernigan had grown up around the Fort. The name came from the Jernigan family, early settlers in the area. By 1850, Jernigan had a post office, and by 1856 the community had expanded northward, and changed its name to Orlando.

There are many theories as to **how Orlando got its name**, but the one is that a man named Orlando Reeves owned a sugar mill and plantation north of Orlando. He carved his name in a tree near what is now Lake Eola. Later settlers assumed the tree was a grave marker. Their speculations as to the carving's origin led to the various accounts of Seminole War battles, and the area around the tree became known as **"Orlando's Grave"** or simply **"Orlando."**

The history of Orlando since the end of the Seminole Wars has been one of pretty steady growth. Shortly before the Civil War, Orlando became the seat of newly created Orange County. It was a quiet country town during the war, but had a population explosion in the years from 1875 to 1895. In that 20 year period, Orlando became the center of Florida's citrus industry.

The "Great Freeze" of 1894-1895 forced many small owners to give up their groves. Owners of bigger groves added to their holdings, and they became "citrus barons". Many of them bought land and expanded their operations south of Orlando in the area around Lake Wales.

Modern times really began in 1956 when **Martin Marietta** opened an aerospace plant and quickly became a major employer. The aerospace program at nearby **Cape Kennedy** also boomed in those years and many Orlando residents drove to the coast every day to work on the moon project. And of course, in October 1971, **Walt Disney World** opened 20 miles southwest of Orlando and changed the course of history in central Florida.

The **Beachline Expressway** allows easy access to **Port Canaveral**, an important cruise ship terminal.

Because of its proximity to the Space Coast near the Kennedy Space Center, many high-tech companies have shifted to the

Orlando area. Many of them also like being close to the research and teaching resources of the University of Central Florida, now the largest university in the state.

But the old charm of Orlando still remains in spite of this commercial progress. It is a city bejeweled by lakes. The street grid pattern is constantly meandering around lakes. The streets are lined and canopied with ancient oaks draped with Spanish moss. A GPS in Orlando is useful if you know the address of your destination. If not, just enjoy the scenic ride. Orange Avenue is the beautiful main north-south drag in Orlando. It starts in the rural areas south of town near Taft and passes through the busy downtown business district on its way to Winter Park.

Many of the neighborhoods surrounding downtown Orlando were created during the 1920's land boom. Most of these areas have been "gentrified" with wonderful streetscaping. Private residents have restored many of the houses, and these neighborhoods are great places to live and visit. **College Park, Delaney Park, Lake Eola Heights, Lancaster Park, Thornton Park** and **Orwin Manor** are just a few of these lovely Orlando Florida communities. Each of these neighborhoods is a quiet oasis close to vibrant downtown Orlando.

Another oasis is Lake Eola in the center of downtown Orlando. This lake and its beautiful surrounding public park have always been a part of City's culture. A beautiful fountain in the center of the lake is lighted at night, and a bandshell offers a venue for musical concerts. Orlando's slogan before Disney was "Orlando, The City Beautiful". It still resonates today.

ORLANDO HOTELS

The major concentration of hotels in Orlando is around Walt Disney World, SeaWorld and Universal Studios. There are many family hotels in Orlando, fine places to stay if you are visiting the theme parks. I will also tell you about some nice places to stay in Orlando that are a bit removed from the parks and their activity.

Grand Bohemian Hotel. This is a small five star experience in the heart of downtown Orlando. It is within walking distance of all downtown attractions, and a place to stay if you want to be pampered. 325 S. Orange Ave., Orlando Florida. 32801. Tel: 407-313-9000.

Embassy Suites Orlando Downtown. Very nice place, not as pricey as the Grand Bohemian but right in the heart of downtown. 191 East Pine Street, Orlando Florida 32801. Tel: 407-841-1000.

Park Plaza Hotel. Okay, I know Winter Park is a separate town from Orlando, but it is close by. I love this little 28 room hotel. It is full of antiques and 1920's charm. When I worked at Universal Studios, our California executives loved this place. 307 Park Avenue South Winter Park, Florida 32789. Tel: 407-647-1072.

The Courtyard At Lake Lucerne. On the edge of downtown, quiet neighborhood. A couple of buildings with a total of 30 rooms. Some are in the former mansion of Dr. Philip Phillips, an Orlando legend. He was one of Florida's biggest citrus barons, and a world class philanthropist. 211 North Lucerne Circle East, Orlando Florida 32801. Tel: 407-648-5188. Book this B&B or others in Orlando now! /li>

ORLANDO RESTAURANTS

There are many fine restaurants at or near the major Orlando theme parks. On this website, however, I will tell you about some of the lesser known but popular Orlando restaurants. If you happen to be a member of Club Corp, the Citrus Club in Orlando is, in my opinion, one of the best restaurants in town. It is a private club, or I would have it listed below with my favorite Orlando restaurants.

Flame Kabob, Dr. Phillips Marketplace on Sand Lake Road

Greek Taverna. Sand Lake Road, Doctor Phillips.

Saffron Indian Restaurant. Sand Lake Road, Doctor Phillips.

Yellow Dog Eats. West of Orlando in Gotha, near Windermere.

ORLANDO ATTRACTIONS

Other travel guides can tell you everything you need to know about Walt Disney World, Universal Studios, SeaWorld and the other major Central Florida tourist attractions. I will focus instead on a few Orlando places that the average tourist will never see.

Harry P. Leu Gardens. This is a wonderful place to get back to nature. It has a formal rose garden, a butterfly garden, herb and vegetable garden, and plenty of camellias and azaleas. Harry P. Leu's historic home is also available for tours. Harry was a successful Orlando businessman. 1920 N. Forest Ave., Orlando Fla 32803. Tel: 407-246-2620. You will learn more about Leu Gardens later in this guide.

Orlando Museum of Art. Tremendous collections of African art and art of the ancient Americas, along with modern American art by artists such as John Singer Sargent, Georgia O'Keeffe, Ansel Adams, Robert Rauschenberg and others. 2416 N Mills Ave, Orlando Fla 32803. Tel: 407-896-4231.

Orlando Science Center. The Orlando Science Center is a favorite of local kids. It encourages curiosity, innovation and discovery. It pulls together all of Central Florida's cultures through participative programs that foster an appreciation for the importance of science and technology to our way of life. It does this by being fun. 777 East Princeton St., Orlando Fla 32803. Tel: 407-514-2000.

ORLANDO LOCATION MAP

Sebring

Sebring is in deep south Central Florida, many miles from an Interstate highway and the tourist attractions and theme parks of Orlando. It is located on the central Florida ridge with some of the highest elevations in south Florida. Sebring is on **US-27** about 170 miles northwest of Miami and 86 miles northeast of Fort Myers.

Sebring is near **Highlands Hammock State Park**, a popular attraction and beautiful example of natural old Florida. The park is a great place to camp while visiting Sebring, Lake Placid and the nearby scenic highways.

History of Sebring Florida

Sebring is on the eastern shore of Lake Jackson in the Ridge Area of southern Central Florida. The land for the town was purchased in 1911 by **George E. Sebring**, a pottery manufacturer from Sebring, Ohio. Mr. Sebring planned a city on the principle of the mythological Grecian city of Heliopolis, the "city of the sun".

The town was designed and built with streets radiating outward from a central park representing the sun. Surveys were made and construction began on the town in 1912, a few months before the arrival of the Atlantic Coast Line Railroad.

The city grew quickly as the citrus industry thrived in this part of Florida. The first setback to the town came in 1917 when a freeze killed or damaged many groves in the area. These groves were replanted, and the town continued to grow steadily until the real estate boom of 1924-1925.

Sebring survived the land boom collapse, and continued to grow slowly when it became the county seat of Highlands County. The county was formed in 1921 from part of DeSoto County and is named for the high sand ridge that forms this part of Florida.

Sebring is the home of the **Sebring International Raceway**, created on a huge former World War Two Army Air Force base. It was first used for car races in 1950. It hosted the 1959 Formula One United States Grand Prix, but is currently best known as the host of the **12 Hours of Sebring**, an annually held American Le Mans Series race.

The house at 2701 Northeast Lakeview Drive where novelist **Rex Beach** committed suicide is located on one of Sebring's main lakes, Lake Jackson.

SEBRING HOTELS

Quality Inn & Suites Conference Center, 6525 US Hwy 27 North, Sebring, Florida 33870. 863-385-4500. Nice clean accommodations, reasonable rates, conveniently located.

Kenilworth Lodge, 836 SE Lakeview Dr, Sebring, Florida 33870. Tel: 863-385-0111. This is a historic inn overlooking Sebring's Lake Jackson. Constructed in 1916 by City of Sebring founder George Sebring, the Kenilworth is one of the finest examples of Mediterranean-Revival architecture in Florida. It has been restored with resort amenities, including golf. Villas and efficiencies, lodge rooms, apartments and suites. All accommodations include mini-fridges, voice mail, individual A/C units and television with 5 free premium movie channels and 6 dedicated sports channels. **Portions of the hotel were closed for renovation in 2016, so make sure to check for updates.**

SEBRING RESTAURANTS

Sunset Grill, 2650 US Highway 27 South, Sebring, Florida 33870. 863-471-3900. A local favorite, this little place is on the shore of Lake Jackson and serves a great meal.

Cowpoke's Watering Hole, 6813 US Hwy 27 South, Sebring, Florida 33870. 863-382-4554. Noted for good steaks and seafood and country-western dancing, it is a favorite of locals.

SEBRING ATTRACTIONS

Harder Hall is an unoccupied hotel located on Little Lake Jackson at 3300 Golfview Drive. It is on the **National Register of Historic Places**. The hotel was designed in the Spanish Colonial Revival Style and has 134 room. Several developers have tried to renovate the hotel over the years, but it is currently (2015) not operating and can't be entered by the public.

Sebring International Raceway, located adjacent to Sebring Regional Airport, is America's premier sports car racing facility.

The **Murals of Lake Placid**. This little town about 16 miles south of Sebring has a downtown area loaded with murals. These picturesque works of art portray various Highlands County historical and cultural events.

SEBRING LOCATION MAP

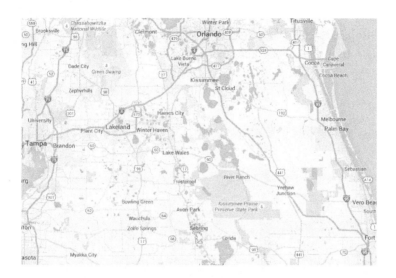

St Cloud

St Cloud is about 5 miles east of Kissimmee on U.S. Highway 192. Much of the business activity in both towns is centered along this highway. The average tourist staying in the area and mainly interested in Walt Disney World, Universal Studios and the other big attractions will hardly be aware of the real St Cloud. It is only when you get off the highway and go into the town that you will be able to enjoy the small town charm.

This town of 35,000 people is on the south shore **of East Lake Tohopekaliga.** Most local folks call it East Lake Toho. It is a round lake about 4 or 5 miles in diameter with marshy shores known for its good fishing. The historic downtown area and City Hall are 4 blocks north of U.S. 192. Pennsylvania Avenue is one of the main streets leading north into downtown. Most of the historic old buildings in St Cloud are along 9th and 10th Streets.

History of St Cloud

Hamilton Disston of Philadelphia bought 4,000,000 acres of Florida land for $1,000,000 shortly after the Civil War. The State sold the land to help pay off its Civil War debts. It was claimed at the time to be the largest private land sale in the history of the world. Disston was also to receive a percentage of additional land if he could drain it. He began to dig canals around St Cloud and Kissimmee, and in 1886 he built the St Cloud sugarcane plantation. Some locals say he named it after the town in Minnesota; others claim he named it after the town in France.

Disston build railroads to haul his products to market, but the Great Freeze of 1894 and 1895 destroyed the plantation. Others tried to raise rice on the plantation, but that didn't work either. So the land lay unproductive and lonely for many years.

In 1909, a development company bought 35,000 acres for the site of a **Grand Army of the Republic** veteran's colony. The Grand Army of the Republic was a huge fraternal organization formed in 1866 and composed of veterans of the **Union Army** who had served in the Civil War. The town was laid out on the south shore of East Lake Toho. Many of the north-south streets were named after the states from which the Union Army veterans had served. This heritage has been retained in the street names of today.

St Cloud Florida was incorporated in 1915, and the downtown areas still feature historic old buildings from that era. In addition to the interesting downtown section, St Cloud has developed a beautiful park on the south shore of Lake Toho. The park includes walking and biking trails and a nice marina.

The town has abundant large trees including many ancient oaks. There are all kinds of homes that date back to the boom days of the 1920s; many of them have been fixed up and are as charming as any homes in the State of Florida.

Religious Controversy. For many years there was a lighted cross on the top of St Cloud's water tower on the south side of the main drag, U.S.-192. It was a landmark that many Floridians enjoyed as they drove through town. The cross was an obvious symbol of the first name of the town, **SAINT**.

In 1987, the **ACLU** filed a lawsuit on behalf of a resident who objected to the cross. The lawsuit said thecross display was unconstitutional because it promoted one religion and was on city property. The City tried to compromise by replacing the old cross with a Greek cross; it didn't work, the ACLU prevailed and the cross on the water tower is gone forever.

Many of the old buildings in the historic district have been decorated with murals of historic significance. Each mural has a plaque that describes the moment in history portrayed by the mural.

ST CLOUD RESTAURANTS

The Catfish Place, 2324 13th Street, St. Cloud, Florida 34769. Tel: 407-892-5771. The best place in town for fresh catfish, brought in daily from Lake Okeechobee.

ST CLOUD LOCATION MAP

Tavares

Tavares Is a town of 14,000 people about 35 miles northwest of Orlando. Along with **Eustis** and **Mount Dora**, it is one apex of what is known as Florida's "Golden Triangle". Tavares is the county seat of Lake County.

Tavares was founded in 1880 by **Alexander St. Clair Abrams**, a railroad and newspaper executive. He named the town after one of his Portuguese ancestors. Abrams initially sought to develop the town as a tourist destination, but later made the decision that its location would result in it becoming a great industrial and railroad center and the capital of Florida.

He spent at least $500,000 building a large hotel, lumber mills, stores, a cigar factory and railroad lines. Streets and avenues were named after Abrams' relatives and friends. The Duke of

Sutherland and other British noblemen stayed at Abrams' hotel, **The Peninsular**.

A large part of Tavares was destroyed in a fire in 1888, and a few years after that the great freeze of 1895 and 1896 caused the town to be nearly abandoned.

One of the existing reminders of the old days in Tavares is the Union Congregational Church at 302 St. Clair Abrams Avenue. The church was built in 1888 on land donated by Mr. Abrams.

Citrus made a comeback and has been a staple of the community for many years. Tavares is at the west end of Lake Dora, and boating and seaplanes are an important part of the town's ambiance.

The chain of lakes including Lakes Dora, Harris, Griffin and Eustis are connected by canals and give boaters access to the St Johns River and ultimately the Atlantic Ocean.

The downtown area has been redeveloped with many nice shops and restaurants, and a seaplane base makes for some entertaining flights in Central Florida.

Some Tavares restaurants are listed earlier in the **Mount Dora** restaurants page.

TAVARES LOCATION MAP

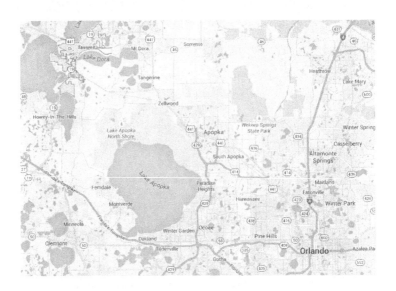

The Villages

The Villages Florida is a master planned retirement community that sprawls over Sumter, Lake and Marion counties along US-441/US-27 between Ocala and Leesburg. It is about 68 miles northwest of Orlando International Airport and about 90 miles northeast of Tampa International Airport. The Villages is bounded approximately on the east by US 27/US 441, on the west by US-301, on the north by County Road 42 and on the south by Sumter County Road 466A.

Sumter **County Road 466** serves as the main east-west corridor, with **Buena Vista Boulevard** and **Morse Boulevard** serving as major north-south corridors.

HISTORY OF THE VILLAGES FLORIDA

Harold Schwartz, a Michigan businessman, began selling land tracts via mail order in the area in the 1960's. Not too long after, the laws were changed to prohibit selling real estate by mail. It started to develop in earnest in the 1980's when Schwartz brought in **H. Gary Morse** to run the operation. Morse had a gift for understanding what active retirees were looking for in a lifestyle, and he made sure The Villages had those factors.

He was wildly successful, and The Villages Florida has altered forever the backroads travel pattern in this part of the state. The Villages Florida now has about 77,681 people according to the 2010 census, and most experts predict the population will continue to increase until there are no more lots to sell or nearby land to develop.

The population in the 2000 census was only 8,333, so it is obvious that people are attracted to the community in overwhelming numbers.

GENERAL INFORMATION ABOUT THE VILLAGES

Most of The Villages is an "adults only" community where homes must be occupied by at least one person who is 55 years of age or older. Persons under the age of 19 years are not permitted to reside within The Villages but may visit for a maximum of 30 days per year.

There are three subdivisions in The Villages which are designated as family units and are not subject to this restriction.

I know many people who live in The Villages, and all of them love the place. Most of them are active retirees who came down from up north, and most of them are very conservative both socially and politically.

I personally don't know any native Floridians who live in The Villages, although I am sure there must be some. Its appearance has made it become the quintessential "Anywhere, USA". If you were to be brought there blindfolded and then allowed to see it, you'd think you were in any number of southern states. The only thing "Florida" about The Villages is the climate and the golf courses.

The Villages comprises several communities, each clustered around one of 37 separate golf courses. 28 of these courses are 9 hole executive layouts, and 9 of them are country club 18 hole championship courses.

One of the benefits of living there is that you can play golf "free" for the rest of your life on the 9 hole courses. Your golf membership is included in the general fees that a homeowner pays in local taxes to a Community Development District. Greens fees are charged on the 18 hole courses.

Community Development Districts are not uncommon in Florida; there are more than 200 of them. They are quasi-governmental units that give the developer the right to finance his development with bonds and pass on the cost of infrastructure to the eventual residents of the district.

LIFESTYLES IN THE VILLAGES

Many - if not most - people who live in The Villages have a golf cart. CBS's "Sunday Morning" television show in May 2011 said there are 50,000 carts. Grocery stores, restaurants, health spas, and most other businesses can be reached by using a golf cart. If you're a visitor, you can even rent a golf cart at several locations.

There are two town squares in The Villages, each with a band shell and free concerts. These squares are the hubs of community evening activity. Thousands of golf carts line up while their occupants enjoy the music and fellowship and head home when it's done.

Some of them are very cute, fixed up to look like miniature Rolls Royces, fire engines, boats or whatever strikes the owner's fancy.

The Villages has hundreds of miles of golf cart paths; golf carts are the preferred means of transportation for many residents, even those who don't play golf.

The Villages residents enjoy more than 1300 clubs that cover just about any hobby or interest a person could have. They also have sports teams and leagues and all kinds of other activities that are free to the residents. Everybody who lives there seems to be having fun.

Speaking of fun, there have been rumors that The Villages has the highest rate of STD (sexually transmitted diseases) in the United States of America. My friends who live in the community tell me this rumor is nothing more than an urban myth. I have not researched this either in person or on line.

THE CHANGING TIMES

Some of the local Floridians who lived in Sumter, Lake and Marion counties before The Villages was developed have a real love-hate relationship with the community. They love the jobs and money that it brings into their lives, but they feel slighted and discriminated against by the residents of The Villages.

There are some Florida crackers who insist that most of the residents of The Villages would like the entire place to be a gated community to keep "outsiders" like them from coming in.

For what it's worth, during my more than 50 years in Florida I have observed people who already live here resenting it when other people move in. It seems to be true whether they are Florida natives or recent transplants from the north. Many people want to slam the door shut after they've moved to Florida.

THE VILLAGES FLORIDA HOTELS

Hotels in and around The Villages are generally very new and modern, with reasonable rates.

Here are my 3 favorite places to stay when I visit The Villages:

Comfort Suites The Villages, 1202 Avenida Central, Lady Lake, FL 32159. Tel: 352-259-6578. This is a modern, quiet and comfortable place close to everything in The Villages. You will feel right at home. It's right next door to the Holiday Inn Express, another place I recommend. Average rate $110-111.

Hampton Inn and Suites, 11727 NE 63rd Drive, The Villages, FL 32162. Tel: 352-259-8246. This modern place is very clean and comfortable and is close to everything in The Villages. The staff is also very helpful and can answer any of your questions about the area. Average rate $80-$126

Holiday Inn Express Hotel & Suites, 1205 Avenida Central North, Lady Lake, Florida 32159. Tel: 877-859-5095. This new motel is very clean and comfortable and near everything you will want to see in The Villages. It is not far from the other two hotels. Average rate $98-$109.

There are also hotels and some bed and breakfast inns nearby in the small Florida towns of Lady Lake, Leesburg, Ocala and

Wildwood. A bit further away, but within an easy drive are Mount Dora, Gainesville and several other towns. Most people who visit The Villages, however, tend to want to stay there to look at property and check out the place's amenities.

RESTAURANTS IN THE VILLAGES.

A great source for learning about restaurants is the website of the **The Villages In and Out Gourmet Club (thevillagesgourmetclub.com/).** Local volunteers have reviewed several hundred restaurants in and near The Villages. One of my favorite restaurants near The Villages is the **Cotillion Southern Café** in nearby **Wildwood**. You have to take a car, however, it's too far for golf carts.

THE VILLAGES LOCATION MAP

Wauchula

Wauchula is a pretty little country town of about 5,000 people located in Hardee County. The county is named for the 23rd Governor of Florida, **Cary A. Hardee**, who lived a good long life and died in 1957. He wasn't from the area, however, he was from Live Oak in North Florida.

Wauchula is the County Seat, and for many years has been called the **"Cucumber Capital of the World"**. These days watermelons and citrus are even more important to the local economy.

The area around Wauchula was settled primarily to support Fort Hartsuff, one of the many U.S. Army forts in Florida during the Seminole Wars. When the Florida Southern Railway came to the area in 1886, they built a depot and named the town Wauchula.

The name comes from a Miccosoukee Indian word "wa-tu-la-ha-kee", meaning "call of the sand hill crane".

The town was incorporated in 1902, and the historic City Hall was built in 1926. Like most of the old Florida towns along the Peace River, Wauchula depended heavily on the phosphate industry, free range cattle and citrus groves.

The City Hall and train depot are still standing, and are among the buildings that give Wauchula its special brand of small town charm blended with history and heritage.

Wauchula is the home of the pioneer Carlton family. The name of Carlton is prominent in Wauchula ranching, banking and politics. **Doyle Elam Carlton** was born in Wauchula and rose through state politics to become the 25th Governor of Florida.

His descendants have also been prominent in Florida politics and agriculture. His son, Doyle E. Carlton, Jr., was a successful rancher and a Florida state senator for ten years. He also made a try for election as Governor of Florida.

Wauchula still has a lot of Southern charm and a laid back lifestyle. It is just far enough from the glitz and glamour of Tampa, Orlando and Sarasota to have retained its Old Florida charm.

WAUCHULA LOCATION MAP

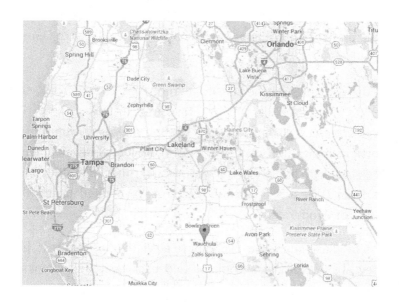

Windermere

Windermere is one of the nicest small towns in Florida. About 2,000 people live among the large oaks located on an isthmus on the Butler Chain of Lakes west of Orlando. Founded in 1889, Windermere is one of the oldest communities in Orange County.

By 1910, the Windermere Improvement Company had been formed, homes were built and thousands of acres of citrus planted all around the area. Many of these old homes and buildings have been preserved and add to the charm of this little place nestled among the old oaks and clear lakes of Central Florida.

In the early days of the construction of Walt Disney World, the 1960's and 1970's, many Disney executives lived in Windermere, including **Don Edgren**, **Bob Allen** and **Admiral Joe Fowler**. In more recent years, plush golf course developments like Isleworth, home of **Tiger Woods** and other celebrities such as **Shaq O'Neal** and **Michael Eisner** have popped up on the edges of Windermere.

Maybe these fancy new places have a Windermere address, but they are far removed from the laid back beautiful homes of what I guess I'll call "old Windermere".

Windermere's location on the isthmus puts it on the shortest path between the east and west sides of the chain of lakes. The next lake crossing to the south is 7.5 miles away at Lake Buena Vista where CR-535 and Apopka-Vineland Road intersect. The next lake crossing to the north is at Gotha, 2 miles north.

This has made Windermere a busy little place for traffic, but the town has handled it beautifully with roundabouts and other traffic calming techniques.

They don't mind handing out speeding tickets, either.

An interesting little place to see while you are in town is the **Windermere School**. It is on the **National Register of Historic Places**. It is located at 113 West Seventh Avenue. Just park your car and walk right up to it and take a picture like I did.

Windermere is a pleasant and peaceful place to spend a day; you won't feel like speeding through this pretty little town. Although the main drag is paved, most of the residential streets are not. The residents want it that way and have resisted many times the efforts of some to lay down asphalt.

Very few tourists venture off the paved road into the unknown of the dirt trails that lead off through the tree canopies to who knows where. Most folks do not want to take the road less traveled; Windermere folks seem to know that and treasure and protect their solitude.

Stop and buy some wine at **Tim's Wine Market** or go down the road to **Gotha** for lunch at **Yellow Dog Eats**. Tim's doesn't sell wine by the glass. They allowed me to buy a bottle and drink some of it at their big guest table while watching a World Cup soccer match.

WINDERMERE LOCATION MAP

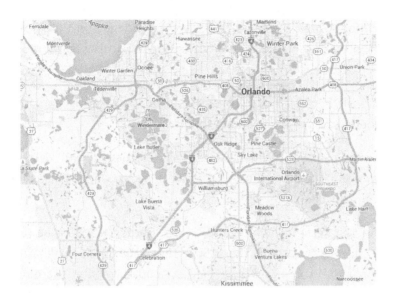

Winter Garden

Winter Garden is about 14 miles west of Orlando on State Road 50 in western Orange County. Its population is slightly more than 30,000.

One of the first things a new Floridian has to do is learn the whereabouts of the **"winter" towns**:

Winter Garden, Winter Park, Winter Haven and Winter Springs. I'll even mention Winter Beach over near Sebastian, but not many people remember it these days.

The first settlers came to the Winter Garden Florida area just before the Civil War in the 1850's. They established small farms along the south shore of Lake Apopka. Winter Garden's economy depended largely on citrus and vegetable production. This economy was helped when the **Orange Belt Railroad** was completed and came through town. By 1900, a small commercial district had popped up along Plant Street and residential neighborhoods began to appear on the side streets.

There are still many historic buildings in Winter Garden, most of them dating back to the period from 1915 to 1940. Many of the old railroad routes were combined into **The West Orange Trail**, a 22-mile long multi-use rail trail owned by Orange County.

The trail passes through downtown **Oakland, Winter Garden**, and **Apopka**. It is very popular with walkers, joggers and bicyclists.

At one time, especially in the 1930's, Winter Garden's location on **Lake Apopka** made it a fisherman's paradise. Lake Apopka is the second largest lake in Florida, trailing only Lake Okeechobee in size. Some of the best bass fishing in the United States was to be had in the clean waters of Lake Apopka. Winter Garden Florida was the center of this fishing activity.

Huge agricultural operations along the northern shores of Lake Apopka resulted in toxic runoff into the lake and its glory days as a fishing paradise are lost in the distant past. There are ongoing efforts to buy up the farms and improve the water quality of this beautiful lake. There has been some success with this effort, and we should all keep our fingers crossed.

Historic downtown Winter Garden contains an eclectic collection of restaurants, shops, cafes, a train depot that is now a museum, and a theater. Brick paving, tree planters and benches make this a favorite spot for locals and tourists to visit.

A few blocks north of downtown Plant Street are several public parks, a public swimming pool and community center. This area also has a large city owned trailer park called **Trailer City** that opened in 1936 and is home to a couple of hundred happy people.

Oakland is a small town of about 2,500 people just west of Winter Garden Florida. It is also on the southern shore of Lake Apopka and a stop on the West Orange Trail.

The town was once the center of this entire region of Central Florida. It was a railroad town, and many railroad people lived among the oak filled village streets. The town today is quiet and peaceful, and is a good example of the Old Florida so many of us miss. It's a short two mile drive from Winter Garden to Oakland. You will see some beautiful houses along the way.

Oakland began to boom when the Orange Belt Railroad came through town in the 1880's. The biggest shareholder in that railroad was **Peter Demens**, who ended up running the railroad to St. Petersburg. He named St. Pete after his hometown in Russia.

Oakland's economic fortunes declined when the railroads pulled out of town more than 100 years ago. The freezes of 1894 and 1895 killed most of the groves, and the railroads had nothing to ship. The route of the original railroad is now the West Orange Trail, a favorite of walkers and hikers from everywhere.

Then along came a fire in the late 1890's that destroyed most of the downtown.

Some people don't miss the booming old days in Oakland and prefer the quiet serenity that now prevails. You will enjoy a visit to this quiet little Old Florida town.

Ocoee is a small town on the east side of Winter Garden Florida. It was founded by Dr. J. D. Starke in the 1850's who brought his slaves into Central Florida and established a camp on the north shore of a lake that later became known as Lake Starke for obvious reasons.

Starke and most of his group had contracted malaria, and were looking for a healthier environment when they came upon the lake. They got healthier and settled permanently in the area. The town was originally called Starke Lake, but changed its name later to Ocoee.

The Florida Midland Railroad came to town in the 1880's, and the little village began to boom. After the American Civil War, a former confederate soldier named Captain Bluford Sims from Tennessee moved to the area and began planting citrus. Nobody is sure where the name of the town came from, but some have speculated it is named after an Ocoee in Tennessee.

One of the still existing structures from the glory days of Ocoee is the Ocoee Christian Church, an example of Carpenter Gothic architecture at 15 South Bluford Avenue. It is on the U.S. National Register of Historic Places. It was built in 1891.

WINTER GARDEN LOCATION MAP

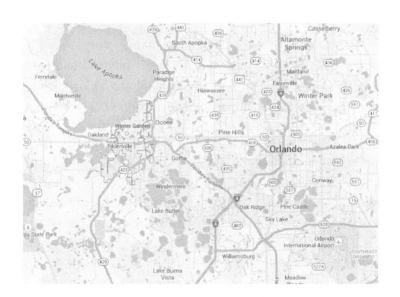

Winter Haven

Winter Haven was defined for years by the presence of **Cypress Gardens**, one of the earliest Florida tourist attractions. Cypress Gardens opened on January 2, 1936 and was the brainchild of Dick Pope, Sr. and his wife Julie. It became one of the biggest tourist attractions in Florida in the days before Walt Disney World came along.

It was known as the "Water Ski Capital of the World" because it was the center of that new and popular sport. Many movies were filmed at Cypress Gardens, including a few by the popular swimming star Esther Williams. This world famous attraction featuring Southern Belles and talented water skiers operated from 1936 to 2009, finally closing its doors to be reborn in 2011 as the newest and largest **Legoland** amusement park in the world.

Legoland offers a unique mix of more than 50 rides, shows and attractions, including spectacular Lego models and other interactive elements for the whole family to enjoy together. They have also preserved key elements of the beloved Cypress Gardens.

Winter Haven has always been a unique Florida town, with or without Cypress Gardens and Legoland. The town is off the interstate highways in the rolling Central Florida land between Orlando and Tampa. Many tourists miss Winter Haven because it is not on the interstate route. A scenic Florida backroads travel route is to exit I-4 a few miles west of US-27 and go south on County Road 557 through Lake Alfred. Then catch US-17 and go south all the way to Winter Haven. The town is about 11 miles south of I-4.

It is nestled among 50 lakes, of which 24 are connected by navigable canals. The entire system, known as the "Chain Of Lakes", is a boater's paradise. Winter Haven is known as The **Chain of Lakes City.** It is a close knit community of 34,000 people, and has preserved many of its historic houses and neighborhoods.

The main campus of the four-year **Polk State College** is located in Winter Haven.

Winter Haven is a good place to stage a Florida vacation. Historic Bok Tower and Gardens is in nearby Lake Wales, and Fantasy of Flight Air Museum is just down the road. Busch Gardens in Tampa and the Orlando attractions - Walt Disney World, SeaWorld and Universal Studios - are about an hour away.

WINTER HAVEN LOCATION MAP

Winter Park

Winter Park is an upscale town of about 30,000 people in the heart of Orlando's urban area. It's sometimes hard to believe such a quiet place exists so near to the bustle of Walt Disney World and Universal Studios. The town is often overlooked as a central Florida tourism attraction, but is definitely worth a visit or an extended stay. Its **Park Avenue** shopping district is a wonderful place to spend a day or a week.

I lived in Winter Park on two separate occasions. It is a relaxing place to live. If you live close to downtown, everything you need is within walking distance. Shops and restaurants line the brick paved Park Avenue. As the name implies, there is a large grassy tree shaded park along the west side of the avenue – **Central Park**.

Flowers and ferns are cultivated and hanging from balconies all along the avenue. Many of the restaurants have sidewalk dining, and the whole Park Avenue stretch is a people watcher's paradise.

Even the Amtrak station is right downtown across the park on Park Avenue. My son used to take the train down from Georgia and walk to my house to visit me.

Several museums are within walking distance of Park Avenue.

History of Winter Park

David Mizelle bought 8 acres of land in 1858 between the present Lakes Mizelle, Berry and Virginia. He founded the little town of Lake View on his land. In 1879 the name was changed to Osceola. In 1881 Loring A. Chase of Chicago visited the place, loved the area and bought 600 acres along Lake Maitland and Lake Osceola. He and a partner, O.E. Chapman, platted the town and named it Winter Park.

Winter Park began to develop in the 1880s as a citrus-growing center. It became a wintering retreat for wealthy Northerners, including Colonel Franklin Fairbanks and his partner, Charles Hosmer Morse. They visited the area on one of their Florida vacations and fell in love with the place. They were partners in various businesses including what is now the **Fairbanks Morse Company**, manufacturers of engines and pumps. Fairbanks Avenue and Morse Boulevard in Winter Park are named for these gentlemen who contributed much to the development of Winter Park in the early days.

In 1885, the Congregational Church established Florida's first institute of higher learning, **Rollins College**. The college's campus sits on the shore of Lake Virginia. Rollins is considered by most folks to be one of the best Florida colleges.

Anthony Perkins was a student at Rollins before hitting it big as Norman Bates in Hitchcock's 1960 classic, "Psycho". Another Rollins graduate, Donald Cram, won a 1987 Nobel Prize for chemistry. Author **Rex Beach**, who wrote "The Spoilers" and other classics, went to Rollins and his grave is on campus. The architecture of Rollins College inspires visions of Florida's Spanish heritage. The campus is a pleasant place to take a walk.

The **scenic boat tour** at the eastern end of Morse Boulevard takes passengers on tours through the narrow canals between Lakes Virginia and Osceola. They have been at this location since 1938. The tour highlights nature and local birds, but another outstanding feature of the tours are the opulent mansions, old and new, that line the lakes.

Venice of America, Boat Trips through Winter Park, Florida

WINTER PARK MOTELS

Park Plaza Hotel. This is the only hotel right downtown, and is a treat to stay in. Sit on your balcony and watch the people strolling along the avenue. 307 S Park Ave, Winter Park Florida. Tel: 407-647-1072

WINTER PARK RESTAURANTS

Winter Park has so many good places to eat it is tough to decide where to start. When I lived there in a condo two blocks from Park Avenue, there were 17 good restaurants within a short walk.

The restaurant mix changes with the years. Here are a couple of the good ones I know something about that are worth visiting.

310 Park South. Located across Park Avenue from Park Plaza Hotel. Enjoy cafe seating with great view of the avenue. Also has a nice full bar with good wine. 310 Park Avenue South, Winter Park Florida. Tel: 407-647-7277.

Bubbalou's Bodacious BBQ. Not fancy, but some of the best barbecue in Florida. A local tradition. 1471 Lee Rd, Winter Park Florida. Tel: 407-628-1212.

Bosphorous Turkish Cuisine. Enjoy fine mid-eastern dining with kefta, kabobs and all the rest. 108 S Park Ave, Winter Park Florida. Tel: 407-644-8609. Also has Dr. Phillips location.

WINTER PARK ATTRACTIONS

Rollins College. A fine place to take a walk or get a good college degree. Wonderful old buildings with some great Moorish/Spanish architecture.

The Charles Hosmer Morse Museum of American Art. The museum displays the world's most comprehensive collection of works by Louis Comfort Tiffany (1848-1933). The collection includes stained-glass windows, lamps, jewelry and paintings. 445 North Park Avenue, Winter Park. Tel: 407-645-5311.

Scenic Boat Tour. This is a don't miss experience. Pontoon boats with knowledgeable guides take you on a tour of the Winter Park lakes linked by narrow canals. You will glide quietly under live oaks draped with Spanish moss, sabal palms, and dense patches of bamboo stalks and banana trees. The lakefront mansions will boggle your mind. 312 East Morse Blvd., Winter Park. Tel: 407-644-4056

Albin Polasek Museum & Sculpture Gardens. This museum is in the impressive former house of the sculptor. The house was originally owned by Harry Sinclair of the oil company. It is on Lake Osceola. The magnificent building and grounds showcase dozens of classical sculptures by the late Czech-American sculptor. 633 Osceola Avenue, Winter Park. Tel: 407-647-6294.

Winter Park Sidewalk Art Festival. This annual sidewalk art festival is one of the best in the country. It takes place along Park Avenue every year. The festival is held on the third weekend in March. More than 350,000 people usually flock to this show to view the work of over 1200 artists.

WINTER PARK LOCATION MAP

BEACHES

There are no ocean beaches in Central Florida, but there are miles of freshwater lake shorelines. There is also a long stretch of shoreline along the St. Johns River. There are a literally thousands of fresh water lakes in Central Florida. Many of them are good for swimming, but it is best to swim in designated areas to be as safe as possible from alligators and water moccasins.

As recently as **August 2015, a woman was seriously injured by an alligator in the Wekiva River** north of Orlando. She was swimming in an area that has plenty of signs warning about alligators. She either didn't see the signs or didn't take them seriously. In any event, she lost an arm to the gator. My advice before swimming in any river or lake or pond in Central Florida is to seek some local advice before jumping in. And always believe signs if they warn of alligators in the area.

Most communities in Central Florida are little more than an hour away from the beautiful white Atlantic beaches. **New Smyrna Beach** and **Cocoa Beach** have long been beach vacation destinations for Orlando natives. Natives of **St. Cloud** and **Kissimmee** would be more likely to enjoy the beaches of **Indialantic, Melbourne Beach** or **Vero Beach**.

Disney has a beach resort in Wabasso north of Vero Beach.

STATE PARKS

There are 14 beautiful Florida State Parks in Central Florida State Parks that offer a large variety of natural experiences and camping opportunities in totally different natural environments. One of my favorite parks is in the far southern part of the region near Sebring. **Highlands Hammock State** Park is a 9,000 acre treasure that will show you more natural Florida than just about any place you can imagine.

Any Central Florida travel adventure will be enhanced by a visit to one of the state parks. Here are addresses and telephone numbers of Central Florida State Parks. The parks that I've listed in **BOLD PRINT CAPITAL LETTERS** have full service campgrounds. Some of the others may have no camping at all, or primitive, equestrian or group camping.

Allen David Broussard State Park Catfish Creek, 3950 Firetower Rd, Haines City. 863-696-1112

Colt Creek State Park, 16000 State Rd 471, Lakeland, **FL** 33809. 863-815-6761

Dunns Creek State Park, 320 Sisco Road, Pomona Park, FL 32181. 386-329-3721

HIGHLANDS HAMMOCK STATE PARK, , 5931 Hammock Road, Sebring, FL 33872 863-386-6094

Hontoon Island State Park, 2309 River Ridge Road, Deland, FL 32720. 386-736-5309

KISSIMMEE PRAIRIE PRESERVE STATE PARK, 33104 NW 192 Ave., Okeechobee .863-462-5360

LAKE GRIFFIN STATE PARK, 3089 U.S. 441-27, Fruitland Park, FL 34731. 352-360-6760

Lake June in Winter Scrub State Park, 5931 Hammock Road, Sebring, FL 33872. 863-386-6099

LAKE KISSIMMEE STATE PARK, 14248 Camp Mack Road, Lake Wales, FL 33853. 863-696-1112

LAKE LOUISA STATE PARK, 7305 US Hwy 27, Clermont, FL 34714. 352-394-3969

Lower Wekiva River Preserve State Park, 1800 Wekiwa Circle, Apopka, FL 32712. 407-884 2008

Paynes Creek Historic State Park, 888 Lake Branch Road, Bowling Green, FL 33834 863-375-4717

Ravine Gardens State Park, 1600 Twigg Street, Palatka, FL 32177. 386-329-3721

Rock Springs Run State Reserve, 1800 Wekiwa Circle, Apopka, FL 32712. 407-884 2008

SILVER RIVER STATE PARK, 1425 NE 58th Avenue, Ocala, FL 34470. 352-236-7148

WEKIWA SPRINGS STATE PARK, 1800 Wekiwa Circle, Apopka, FL 32712. 407-884 2008

TOURIST ATTRACTIONS

There are more tourist attractions in Central Florida than in any other region of the state. This guide will not cover all of them, but will focus on the following attractions:

Bok Tower Gardens, Lake Wales

Dinosaur World, Plant City

Florida Citrus Tower, Clermont

Gatorland, Kissimmee

Leu Gardens, Orlando

Orlando Tree Tour, Orlando

Seaworld, Orlando

Spook Hill, Lake Wales

Universal Studios, Orlando

Walt Disney World, Orlando

Webster Flea Markets, Webster

Most of these are low key attractions that harken back to the **Old Florida** of yesteryear. Seaworld, Universal Studios and Walt Disney World are included just for brief informational purposes. For all attraction, the best source of current information in the attraction's official website.

Bok Tower Gardens

1151 Tower Boulevard
Lake Wales, Florida 33853
863-676-1408
boktowergardens.org

Bok Tower Gardens is a serene sanctuary not far from the hectic pace and noise of typical Central Florida tourist attractions. This place of tranquil beauty is only one hour south of Orlando.

He decided to buy the hill and surrounding acreage, and hired famous landscape architect **Frederick Law Olmstead** to design a garden. He told Olmstead to make the barren Sandhill into "a spot of beauty second to none in the country".

Edward Bok was a Dutch immigrant who became a Pulitzer Prize winning author and an editor. He became famous as the editor of **Ladies Home Journal**, a major magazine in its time. Bok and his wife spent winters at the **Mountain Lake** community near Lake Wales, Florida. He loved to take walks to the top of nearby **Iron Mountain**, the highest hill in the Lake Wales Ridge region of Florida.

Mr. Olmstead succeeded. Today the tropical plantings provide cooling shade to visitors, and refuge for squirrels and more than 100 bird species. It is on many discerning people's list of favorite Florida tourist attractions.

Almost as an afterthought, Bok decided to have a magnificent "singing tower" added to the gardens. It would have a carillon in it, and would be designed to fit well with the gardens. The Bok Tower is built of Florida coquina stone and Georgia pink marble. It contains one of the finest Carillons in the world, with 71 bells. The architecture of the tower with its carvings and mosaics is worth the visit alone and would make this one of the most popular Florida tourist attractions even without the gardens.

The Bok Tower and Gardens were created by Mr. Bok to give thanks to America for the opportunities he was given. Bok Tower Gardens was dedicated on February 1, 1929, by the president of the United States, **Calvin Coolidge**. It is listed on the **National Register of Historic Places** as a National Landmark.

Edward William Bok died in Lake Wales within sight of the Tower on January 9, 1930, and is now buried at the base of the tower.

The carillon plays concerts at 1 and 3 p.m. daily, and brief musical selections throughout the day.

Bok Tower Gardens has become a popular site for weddings, in addition to being one of the major Florida tourist attractions. This sanctuary is an ideal place to go every now and then to renew oneself. Not many Florida tourist attractions can make that claim.

Give quiet thanks to Edward W. Bok when you go.

ADMISSION FEES

There are several different options that can be chosen, starting at $12 for adults and $3 for kids between 5-12. Group rates are available with pre-registration of 20 or more. Saturday admission rate: On 8-9 a.m. on Saturdays, the admission rate is now 50 percent of general admission. General admission tickets are good for one day only and do not include specially ticketed events.

HOURS

Bok Tower Gardens is open every day of the year from 8 a.m. to 6 p.m. with last admission at 5 p.m. The **Visitor Center** is open from 9 a.m. to 5 p.m.

DIRECTIONS TO BOK TOWER GARDENS

From Orlando, take I-4 West. From Tampa, Take I-4 East.

Proceed on I-4 to Exit 55. Take Exit 55 and proceed south on US-27 for approximately 23 miles. Proceed two traffic lights past Eagle Ridge Mall. Turn left on Mountain Lake Cut Off Road. At the caution light, turn right (south) onto County Road 17 also known as Scenic Highway). Proceed on CR 17 for 3/4 miles. Turn left (east) onto Burns Avenue (also known as County Road 17-A). Proceed on Burns Avenue for 1.3 miles. On your left you'll see a main entrance sign to Historic Bok Sanctuary. Turn left and proceed to the entrance gate.

BOK TOWER GARDENS LOCATION MAP

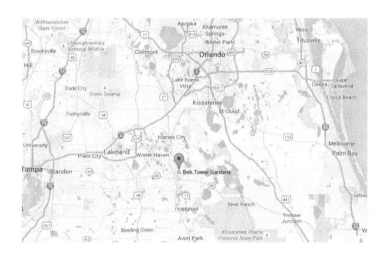

125

Dinosaur World

Dinosaur World
5145 Harvey Tew Road
Plant City, Florida 33565
813-717-9865

The entire family will go "prehistoric" as you explore this most unique of Florida tourist attractions set in a "Jurassic Park" atmosphere! Walk among 150 life-size dinosaur replicas including the notorious "T-Rex" as well as species you never knew existed. This small Florida tourist attraction mixes entertainment with education.

The kids will most likely be talking about this one even after they've visited the other better known Central Florida tourist attractions. For some unknown reason, most kids are crazy about dinosaurs. Maybe they know something we don't about these not obviously loveable creatures from the shadows of prehistory.

Dinosaur Walk is not the only attraction. There is also the Boneyard where you can uncover a life-size dinosaur skeleton. Near the Boneyard is the Fossil Dig where your family can play at being an archaeologist and their newest exhibit, Skeleton Garden with life-size dinosaur skeleton replicas. Other features include the Movie Cave where you can learn about dinosaurs in a subterranean setting, a museum, gift shop and children's playground.

When lunch time comes around the entire family will enjoy snacking with the dinosaurs in the Picnic Area. There is also a nice playground for the kids to enjoy.

This world of dinosaurs is open every day from 900 AM - 500 PM December-January and 900 AM - 600 PM the rest of the year. Check their website for current admission fees.

DINOSAUR WORLD LOCATION MAP

Florida Citrus Tower

141 North US Highway 27
Clermont, Florida 34711.
Telephone: 352-394-4061
CitrusTower.com

The Florida Citrus Tower is on US Highway 27 just north of the intersection of State Road 50 and US-27 in Clermont, Florida. When the tower opened for business in 1956, US-27 was a major divided highway down the sandy central spine of Florida. The highway entered the state north of Tallahassee and meandered through the hills of central Florida all the way down to Miami.

There were no interstate highways in those days and no Florida Turnpike. Tourists traveling down US-27 would stop at Silver Springs, Citrus Tower and Cypress Gardens on their way south.

Florida Citrus Tower
Clermont, FL - 1956

There was no Walt Disney World or Universal Studios in those quieter simpler times when **Dwight D. Eisenhower** was President of the United States and **LeRoy Collins** was Governor of Florida. If you visited Orlando in those days and wanted to go to a Florida tourist attraction, you pretty much had to drive out to Clermont to see the tower.

The tower was built to showcase the hundreds of thousands of citrus trees that covered Central Florida in those days. It was built on one of the highest hills in the central ridge section of Florida and rose 226 feet above the ground. The tip of its highest antenna is 500 feet above sea level.

There is a small gift shop with postcards and tower souvenirs in the building at the base of the tower, along with a large meeting room that is used by local groups. You will see quite a few historic photographs of the way the area used to be. There is an elevator in the gift shop that takes you up 22 stories to the non-air-conditioned glass enclosed observation deck.

The observation deck gives viewers a 360 degree view of the hundreds of lakes and rolling hills in the Clermont area. You can see about 35 miles in any direction from the tower, depending on weather conditions. You are also standing on the highest elevation of any building in Florida.

You won't see many citrus groves. Most of them were destroyed by devastating freezes in the early 1980's and since then most of the land surrounding the tower has been developed into residential subdivisions and shopping mall.

It is still fun, however, to see downtown Orlando and Walt Disney World looming on the distant hazy horizon. A trip to the top of the tower is a voyage back in time to the heyday of citrus in Florida. During the peak of the citrus industry, Lake County Florida produced more citrus than the entire state of California.

INFORMATION AS OF MAY 12, 2016

Hours of Operation: Monday-Saturday, 900am-500pm. Closed on Sundays, Thanksgiving and Christmas.

Admission: (Elevator to top of tower)

Adults $6.00, Children (3-15) $4.00

FLORIDA CITRUS TOWER LOCATION MAP

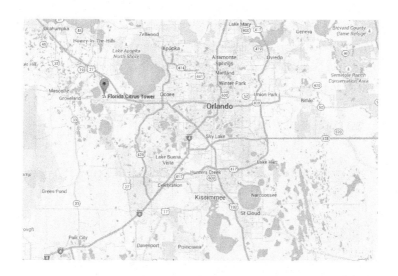

Gatorland

14501 S Orange Blossom Trail
Orlando, FL 32837
(407) 855-5496.
Gatorland.com

Before Mickey Mouse came to Orlando, the main tourist attraction to entertain your kids and visitors was **Gatorland**. Walking through the immense open jaws at the entrance was big fun for a kid - and the adults got a kick out of it, too! I often wonder how many snapshots have been taken of families in those jaws. Also, many pictures were also taken of people or their kids holding gators and snakes.

Back in the day, Gatorland was a free attraction - you were asked to make a donation at the exit. The star exhibit in those days was **"BoneCrusher"** - a 16 ft. Florida Keys crocodile purchased by Gatorland's founder, **Owen Godwin**. The famous publicity photo taken of Godwin and his new acquisition was a tourist publicity icon for many years and the story goes Godwin almost lost his life posing for it!

Another famous photo was one of **Jayne Mansfield** and **Owen Godwin** that hung on the wall of the original gift shop amid the alligator purses and other gator knick knacks.

Gatorland is on 110-acres south of Orlando on U.S. 441 on the way to Kissimmee. The modern park is also a wildlife preserve, and still has an **"Old Florida"** look that the new exhibits and entertainment have not ruined. You will see thousands of alligators and crocodiles including some albino ones. Lots of birds are flying around – not in cages – and a new zip line that will let you soar over all the action. It's called the **Screamin' Gator Zip Line** because you will probably be screaming as you fly over the gators below.

Located between Orlando and Kissimmee on the South Orange Blossom Trail, Gatorland is one of Central Florida's classic attractions, and provides a unique and natural alternative to the larger theme parks of today. Founded by the late Owen Godwin in 1949, and still privately owned by his family today,

There is a wide variety of ticket options available. It's best to go to their website and find out what interests you. Adult general admission tickets are $13.50 for Florida residents and twice that for non-residents. But there are always specials going on, so either call or check the website.

GATORLAND LOCATION MAP

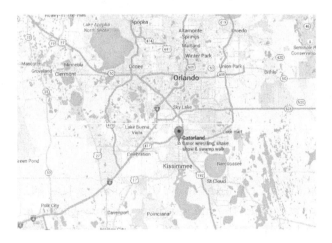

Leu Gardens

1920 North Forest Avenue
Orlando, FL 32803
Tel: 407-246-2620
Leugardens.org

Harry P. Leu Gardens is a 50 acre botanical oasis in north Orlando that has been a leading attraction in the city since 1961. The estate had been owned by several earlier Orlando pioneers including the Mizell family who originally settled on the land in the late 1800s. The next owner was a New Yorker named Duncan Clarkston Pell who bought the land and house in 1902, the same year he married silent movie star Helen Gardner.

The property was finally purchased in 1936 by **Harry P. Leu** and his wife, Mary Jane. Mr. Leu was a native of Orlando who built a successful industrial supply company. He did very well during the development booms in Central Florida.

While Mr. and Mrs. Leu lived on the property, they developed it into a local showplace with gardens featuring roses, camellias and azaleas. Their home, now known as the Leu House Museum, is on the National Register of Historic Places.

The botanical garden is divided into more than a dozen specialty gardens; all of the gardens are connected by nice wide concrete sidewalks. When you enter the **Garden House**, also known as the Welcome Center, the docent tells you what to expect and gives you a map of the gardens and you are off on your own self-guided tour.

The variety of plants you will see on your walking tour is amazing. Make sure to bring your camera. If it is raining, like it was when I last visited, bring your umbrella and snap away in the rain. The photos will still come out okay.

The Floral Clock was inspired by the famous clock of that kind in Edinburgh, Scotland. It is a popular location for small weddings.

You will see gardens devoted to tropical plants like bananas, bird-of-paradise, bromeliads and others that make you feel like you're in a tropical rainforest. Other gardens give you ideas about how you can landscape your own home.

One of the gardens I like is the **Arid Garden**. This features desert plants. No irrigation is used, only natural rainfall, so it gives you good ideas for how to create a drought resistant landscape and save money on your water bill. They even have an herb garden, a citrus grove and a vegetable garden. Some of the harvest is donated to local food banks; other produce is used in some of the cooking classes held in the Garden House.

Another very interesting place is the Palms, Cycads & Bamboo garden. Many of the plants here date back to prehistoric times; it is sometimes called the dinosaur garden.

This quiet oasis is relaxing and mesmerizing. You can hear the faint sounds of traffic on nearby I-4, and the whistle of the Amtrak train on its way to the station in Winter Park. There is a small stream with a waterfall in the Tropical Stream Garden; it's a tranquil place to take a break .

Leu Gardens hosts many events during the year, including outdoor movies and concerts. It is also a popular venue for weddings; they have more than 300 each year. It is also a location for many meetings; nearly 400 meetings are held each year, and it is considered one of the best meeting facilities in Orlando.

All of the signage in the park is QR coded. This means you can use your smart phone to find out more about individual plants on your tour.

HOURS OF OPERATION

Gardens: 9:00 am to 5:00 pm daily (closed Christmas). Last garden admission at 4:30 pm

Leu House Museum Tours: 10:00 am to 3:30 pm daily. (closed during July)

GARDEN ADMISSION FEES

Leu Members: Free

Adults: $10

Child (K-12): $3

Child (4 and under): Free

LEU GARDENS LOCATION MAP

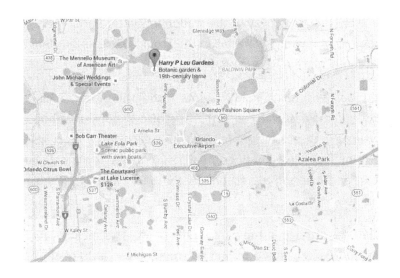

Orlando Tree Tour

The Orlando Tree Tour is a self-guided journey to several City of Orlando parks

You will be on your own and can take as long as you'd like to enjoy these big old trees. Orlando has one of the finest parks

systems in Florida. Many of them can be reserved for private events like weddings or reunions.

The map above from the City of Orlando shows the locations of the parks. The tour begins at No. 1 on the map, and you can

drive from site to site. The only location that requires an admission fee is No. 6, **Harry P. Leu Gardens**.

1. **Mayor Carl T. Langford Park**, 1808 E. Central Boulevard. This park is very close to downtown Orlando and is loaded with many live oaks, laurel oaks and swamp chestnuts.

2. **Dickson Azalea Park**, 100 Rosearden Drive. This park is filled with long leaf pines that tower above the oaks along the ravine. The pines are taller than the oaks in order to be able to reach to the sunshine above the shade of the oaks.

3. **Constitution Green Park**, 300 South Summerlin Avenue. This is a large open grassy park, and near the center of the park is a huge oak tree with branches spreading out and touching the ground. Experts think the tree is between 125 and 175 years old.

4. **Lake Eola Park**, 195 North Rosalind Avenue. This is a large urban park in the middle of Orlando. The park encompasses Lake Eola, a pretty lake with a beautiful fountain in its center.

5. **Big Tree Park**, 930 North Thornton Avenue. This park has what is considered to be the oldest tree in Orlando. Experts indicate the huge live oak is 350 to 400 years old.

6. **Harry P. Leu Gardens**, 1920 North Forest Avenue. The gardens require an admission fee. You will see a natural setting of just about every tree that grows in Florida.

7. **Orlando Loch Haven Park**, 900 E. Princeton Street. The Mayor is the 200 year old live oak that graces the center of this park. There is also lots of statuary and a museum.

www.cityoforlando.net/parks/ is a website with information about the Significant Tree program.

SeaWorld

7007 Sea Harbor Drive
Orlando, FL 32821-8009
Tel: 407-363-2613
Seaworldparks.com/orlando

SeaWorld Orlando is a theme park and marine-life based zoological park just south of Orlando, Florida, that has become one the most popular Florida tourist attractions. It is owned and operated by SeaWorld Parks & Entertainment, a subsidiary of The Blackstone Group.

When combined with its neighbor **Discovery Cove** and the **Aquatica** waterpark, it forms a larger entertainment complex devoted to Earth's oceans and the array of life that inhabits them. Many of the animals, like **Shamu** the killer whale and various trained dolphins are featured in SeaWorld shows in Orlando.

Among SeaWorld's shows are: **Believe - Clyde and Seamore Take Pirate Island - Blue Horizons - Pets Ahoy - A'Lure The Call of the Ocean - Shamu Rocks - Sea Lions Tonite - Reflections - Elmo and Abby's Treasure Hunt - Shamu Christmas...Miracles.**

There are also six rides at SeaWorld, including the tall observation tower called **Sky Tower** that gives you a spectacular view of the theme park and much of Orlando-land. The rides include **Journey To Atlantis, Kraken, Mantis, Wild Arctic Ride** and **Happy Harbor Rides**.

There a many opportunities at SeaWorld for interaction with various animals. In many ways it is an educational experience compared to the other two major theme parks in Orlando.

In 2009, SeaWorld hosted an estimated 5.8 to 6.2 million guests, ranking it the seventh-most visited amusement park in the United States and one of the most visited Florida tourist attractions.

SeaWorld is open every day from 9:00am to 7:00pm. A weekday ticket is $79, but it goes up from there depending on what you want to do. Tickets for Discovery Cove and Aquatica are extra. As in most of the big theme parks, it's best to check their website and buy your tickets online.

Any visit to Orlando will likely include trips to the big three: Walt Disney World, Universal Studios Florida and SeaWorld. These are clearly the most popular Florida tourist attractions

SEAWORLD LOCATION MAP

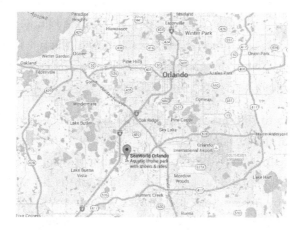

Spook Hill

Spook Hill is located on 5th Street in Lake Wales Florida. It is near an elementary school of the same name and is in the same neighborhood as Bok Tower Gardens. t's a tourist attraction that you can enjoy without leaving your car and without spending a dime.

You park your car at the bottom of the hill and put the gear in neutral. A white line is painted on the road so you know where to park. The car will start rolling uphill. At least that's what you will feel like it's doing.

It is a free attraction, and it has become so popular that the City of Lake Wales has put up direction signs all around town. Just follow the signs until you come to the starting point where the City has placed a big sign that explains the history of the hill. The version on the City's sign is but one tale of many that attempt to explain the mystery of a car rolling up hill.

The hill has been a tourist attraction for many years. Where else can you see gravity being defied? Nobody knows for sure when people started enjoying the mystery of the hill. There are stories of horse drawn wagons enjoying the attraction, so maybe it goes back more than 100 years.

The photo of the sign is from the 1980s. It has been replaced a couple of times since then, but still tells the same story. Another story that the locals tell is that a black man named Buster Coon parked his car at the bottom of the hill and walked to a nearby fishing hole. As he was walking toward his fishing spot, he looked back at his car and saw it rolling up hill. He thought that ghosts were pushing the car, and his story spread all over the town and other people started trying it.

Some folks thought that there was a big magnetic meteor buried beneath the hill that defied the local law of gravity. Many other theories popped up over the years; some credited supernatural causes, others tried to explain the mystery scientifically.

The fact is that the natural terrain and vegetation alongside the road is responsible for the illusion. Don't let that fact spoil your fun. Sometimes it just makes sense to believe your eyes.

A private group has raised money to build a new monument to replace the old sign on the site. The City Council decided the Indian story was the real deal, and approved a conceptual design that includes a Seminole chief and an alligator. The group is now (June 27, 2014) in the process of getting construction permits. They have a website at **www.spookhill.info**/ and a Facebook page.

SPOOK HILL LOCATION MAP

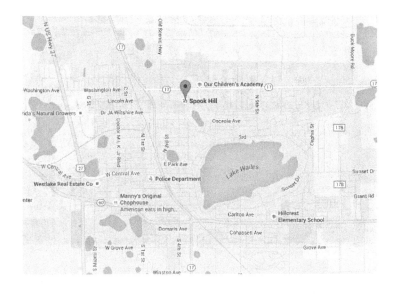

Universal Studios

6000 Universal Boulevard
Orlando, Florida 32819
Tel: 407-363-8000
www.universalorlando.com

Universal Studios Florida, the **Universal Orlando Resort** and **Islands of Adventure** are among the top Florida tourist attractions, second only to Walt Disney World. The original entertainment themed attraction opened to the public in Orlando in the summer of 1990. It very quickly became a success and has continued to expand over the 25 years since it opened. It is a fantastic entertainment park crammed full of television and movie based rides which will wow and amaze you no matter your age.

It is also a current and working TV and movie production facility adding the extra edge that, as you wander around the park, entertainment history could also be being made only a short distance away.

Made up of several distinct parks and areas there are a huge number of attractions on offer. One of the current favorites is the Wizarding **World of Harry Potter**- which has taken J.K. Rowling's phenomenally popular books and created an entire wonderland for guests to explore.

Ms. Rowling first had the inspiration for the Harry Potter stories in 1990, the same year that Universal Studios Florida opened, and published the first book in the series in 1997.

Part of the **Islands of Adventure** district, the Wizarding World of Harry Potter offers shopping in the form of **Honeydukes** sweet store and **Ollivanders** wand store. The **Three Broomsticks** offers great dining.

While walking around the park you'll discover characters and details all inspired by the book. Meanwhile, with rides such as **Flight of the Hippogriff** and **Harry Potter and the Forbidden Journey** you can really get drawn into a magical world and this is an attraction not to be missed. In addition to this latest creation, Universal Studios Florida has a huge range of top attractions which have been inspired by iconic and famed movies. They continually add to these attractions based on the latest movie hits.

Revenge of the Mummy takes you through a thrilling scenario of killing warrior mummies and being confronted with deadly scarab beetles. Rocketing through chambers and tombs at up to

45 miles per hour, this is a ride not to be missed whether you've enjoyed the movies or not.

Men in Black Alien Attack is a great interactive ride allowing you to zap aliens as you cruise through the streets of New York.

Shrek 4-D will let you join Princess Fiona, Shrek and Donkey as you escape Lord Farquaad's ghost.

For some historic film icons, enjoy a 1975 inspired **Jaws** ride; embark on a mission to save the Earth in **Terminator 2**, and zoom across the moonlit sky on a bicycle as you join **E.T.** to save his planet.

Current adult and child admission prices (2016) start at $105 and $100, respectively.

UNIVERSAL STUDIOS LOCATION MAP

Walt Disney World

The goal of this section is to simplify **Walt Disney World Florida** so that the average tourist can figure out what to do and how much it costs. Walt Disney World Florida gets more visitors each year than any other theme park in the world. It can be difficult to figure out how much things cost and what you are going to do. **Not many one day visitors are around anymore**.

This will demystify the Disney ticketing system so you can figure out how much you are going to spend.

There are four theme parks **(Magic Kingdom, Epcot, Animal Kingdom** and **Hollywood Studios**, and two water parks **(Blizzard Beach** and **Typhoon Lagoon**) at Walt Disney World Florida.

Here is some general information about the 4 theme parks and 2 water parks that make up Walt Disney World Florida.

MAGIC KINGDOM

When Walt Disney World Florida opened in October 1971, the Magic Kingdom was the only attraction.

Cinderella's Castle was the centerpiece of this exciting new world. I was there at **Grand Opening** in **October 1971** and still enjoy visiting when my budget allows.

In the early days it was simple figuring out what you wanted to do. There was only the Magic Kingdom, and a general admission ticket cost $3.75. Ride tickets cost from 10 cents to 90 cents per ride and stayed that way throughout the 1970's.

The eight "E" ticket rides at Walt Disney World Florida in the 1970's were:

Pirates of the Caribbean
Jungle Cruise
Country Bear Jamboree
Haunted Mansion
Hall of Presidents
It's a Small World
20,000 Leagues Under the Sea
Space Mountain

All of these original eight, except for 20,000 Leagues Under The Sea, are still operating at Walt Disney World Florida and are very popular. Many other attractions have been added, of course, in the 40 years since the Magic Kingdom opened.

Some of these include:

Astro Orbiter
Big Thunder Mountain Railroad
Buzz Lightyear's Space Ranger Spin
Cinderella Castle
Dumbo The Flying Elephant
Frontierland Shootin' Arcade
Liberty Square Riverboat
Mad Tea Party
Main Street Vehicles
Mickey's PhilharMagic
Monsters, Inc. Laugh Floor
Peter Pan's Flight
Pirates of the Caribbean
Prince Charming Regal Carrousel
Snow White's Scary Adventures
Splash Mountain
Stitch's Great Escape!
Swiss Family Treehouse
The Enchanted Tiki Room
The Hall Of Presidents
The Magic Carpets of Aladdin
The Many Adventures of Winnie the Pooh
Tom Sawyer Island
Tomorrowland® Speedway
Tomorrowland® Transit Authority PeopleMover
Town Square Theater
Walt Disney World® Railroad
Walt Disney's Carousel of Progress

EPCOT

The next major attraction at Walt Disney World Florida was Epcot (**Experimental Prototype Community of Tomorrow**), opening in October 1982. It is built on 300 acres, about twice the size of the Magic Kingdom. Its two major areas are **Future World** and **World Showcase**.

Future World has many attractions along with a lot of shows and other entertainment. Everything in this world is about technology including futuristic ideas. Your adventure at Epcot begins with **Spaceship Earth**, a giant geodesic dome looming over everything else at the park's main entrance.

World Showcase is an area that has pavilions placed around the World Showcase Lagoon. Each pavilion is designed in a style compatible with the typical architecture of the country. Inside are shops, restaurants and other attractions that represent the food and culture of the 11 countries that are included in the Epcot adventure. These countries are:

Mexico
Norway
China
Germany
Italy
United States
Japan
Morocco
France
United Kingdom
Canada

As you walk around Epcot you will see a lot of live performances, including music and dance.

ANIMAL KINGDOM

This Kingdom is loaded with adventure and entertainment that focus on Walt Disney's interest and dedication to conservation and nature. It is a place for animal care, research and education. 1,700 animals representing 250 different species live in Animal Kingdom. Their home is on 500 acres of land specially planted and landscaped to make the animals feel at home and have healthy natural food.

The Animal Kingdom has seven distinct areas:

Oasis
Discovery Island
Camp Minnie-Mickey
Africa
Rafiki's Planet Watch
Asia
Dinoland, U.S.A.

You will see real animals in each area, and will be able to pet some of them. There is also lots of live entertainment and shows.

HOLLYWOOD STUDIOS

The Hollywood studios give you a look at how movies are made. It is like being able to look behind the scenes of a movie set. You will see why Hollywood is often called **"tinsel town"** when you see all the chrome, art deco designs and modern architecture.

You can even be part of the action in the **American Idol Experience**. You can also be in a parade, enter into a rock and roll fantasy experience and enjoy several fantastic attractions.

BLIZZARD BEACH WATER PARK

This and **Typhoon Lagoon** are the two Water Parks in Walt Disney World Resort. Blizzard Beach has one of the tallest and fastest waterslides in the world. There are also tamer attractions for seniors and younger kids.

The Disney tall tale about this place is that it resulted from a freak snow storm that hit Florida. Use your imagination. It became a ski resort, but then it started to melt in the Florida heat. A brave alligator wearing a scarf and hat slid down the ski-jump after the snow was gone, and landed in a pool of melted snow. So now it has become a Florida water park with a ski resort theme.

TYPHOON LAGOON WATER PARK

Typhoon Lagoon has fun for the entire family, including waterslides, raft rides, surf pool with six foot high waves, and a snorkeling reef with real sharks.

The Disney story about Typhoon Lagoon says it came about after a huge mother of all storms. A fishing boat, **Miss Tilly**, still sits on top of **Mount Mayday**, a volcanic mountain, where it was tossed by the storm. Every half hour, the boat's whistle blows and you will see the volcano erupting and trying to throw off Miss Tilly.

Now that the storm is gone, Mount Mayday developed many waterslides and the entire area around the mountain is full of streams, rivers, rapids and slides.

TICKET INFORMATION

The price of a ticket is the same for all four theme parks, and is less for the two water parks.

A **Magic Your Way Base Ticket** gives each person in a visitor party entry to one of the four Theme Parks for one day for each day of the ticket. You have to pick one theme park and stay there for the day.

If you visit more than one day, the per day ticket price gets lower. For example, the average price per day for a 7-day MAGIC YOUR WAY BASE TICKET is less than half the price of the same single-day ticket.

MAGIC YOUR WAY BASE TICKET PRICES FOR A SINGLE DAY AT ONE OF THE FOUR THEME PARKS AS OF MAY 16, 2016

All Guests:

Age 10+......$124

Age 3-9.......$118

Sometimes there are reduced rates for Florida Residents. You need to check with the park in advance:

The two Water Parks at Walt Disney World Florida have a different ticket pricing structure. Again, if you buy a one day ticket you have to choose your water park and stick with it that day. One day ticket prices for Blizzard Beach or Typhoon Lagoon are cheaper, usually a bit more than half the cost of admission to the theme parks.

OTHER TICKET AND PASS OPTIONS

Walt Disney World Resort offers all kinds of ticket options from single day passes to multiple-day passes to annual passes. There are also special deals for Florida residents.

I recommend you go directly to the **Tickets and Passes** page of the Walt Disney World site for current pricing.

HOURS OF OPERATION

The times that the various theme parks and water parks open and close vary with the season. It is best to consult the official Disney website for information

WALT DISNEY WORLD LOCATION MAP

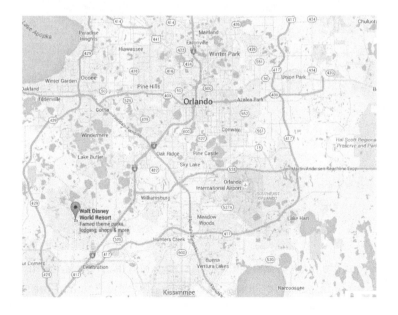

Webster Flea Markets

The **Webster flea markets and farmer's market** are located in the small Central Florida town of the same name. Webster is a very quiet little place except for Mondays. That is the one day of the week when the markets are open.

The Monday thing goes back to the **"blue laws"** which dominated most rural Florida counties back in the bad old days of the Great Depression. One of those laws kept people from doing business on Sunday, so the good ole boys of the area shifted their farmer's market to Monday. The tradition stuck.

During the peak of the winter season, when all of the snowbirds have come down to Florida for the winter, the flea and farmer markets are so busy you have to search awhile for a parking space. It's estimated that as many as **4,000 dealers** are set up on the site, and they receive **100,000 shoppers** on a Monday.

Not nearly as many dealers set up during the hot Florida summers. I made a recent visit in July. I think there were only 400-500 dealers set up. Things being sold were tools, hats, towels, sheets, body lotion, watches, jewelry, perfume, dogs (Yorkies, Chihuahuas and other tiny breeds), rabbits, knives, shirts, dresses and assorted products that reminded me of the offerings in a Dollar store.

A few antiques were displayed here and there, but the biggest antique offerings take place in the cooler winter months.

The Farmer's market had lots of beautiful **tomatoes, onions, peppers, squash, melons, oranges, tangerines** and just about anything else that grows in Florida. There was a large selection of house plants and even **citrus trees**.

There are several Webster flea markets. The biggest one by far is the **Webster Westside Flea Market**. It is said it's the oldest and biggest flea market in Florida. The Sumter County Farmer's Market is across the street just east of the Westside market. There are also a couple of other open shed type flea markets on the same side as the Farmer's Market.

I have found you can park in any of the lots and easily walk around to visit all of the markets. They are all located in one big open field with many of the vendors set up in the shade of big open sheds

There are many concession stands located all over the flea market grounds. You can find hot dogs, hamburgers, kettle corn, peanuts, sandwiches, soft drinks and a lot of other offerings to please the palate.

The town of Webster is very tiny, maybe a few hundred people, so there are only a few shops and restaurants outside of the flea market grounds. One such place I enjoy is **"The Frog In The Window"** at 86 NE 1st Avenue. It is across the street from the public library in the building with the O Boy Bread sign on the side.

The proprietor, **Ken Mueller**, has turned an old hardware building into an eclectic shop featuring a lot of rare and collectible books (his bookstore area is known **as Diddley-Squat's Books**), antiques, and a small coffee shop (The Frog in the Window) where the locals like to gather in the morning. Mr. Mueller knows his local and Florida history, and is also very knowledgeable about baseball history. He's a good guy to swap stories with.

Webster is located just off Exit 61 on I-75. It is located between two major north-south Florida back roads: US-27 and US-301. County Road 471 is a north-south route through town, and State Road 50 is just south of town. It is an easy town to find once you know where to look. The Webster flea markets are on County Road 471 in the middle of town.

HOURS

The Webster Westside flea market hours set the pace for the entire operation.

Summer hours: (June 1 to Sep 30), 600am - 200pm, rain or shine

Winter hours: (Oct 1 to May 31), 500am - 300pm, rain or shine

WEBSTER FLEA MARKET LOCATION MAP

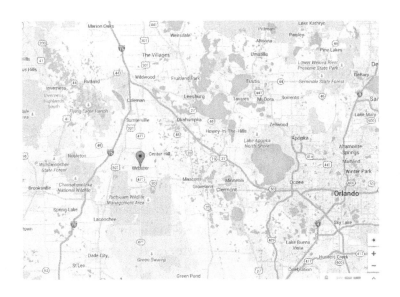

WINERIES

There are 4 Central Florida Wineries listed in this travel guide:

Henscratch Farms Vineyards & Winery, Lake Placid

Hutchinson Farm Winery, Apopka

Lakeridge Winery and Vineyards, Clermont

Whispering Oaks Winery, Oxford

This travel guide will give you detailed information about these wineries.

Henscratch Farms Vineyards and Winery

980 Henscratch Road
Lake Placid, FL 33852
863-699-2060
Henscratchfarms.com

Henscratch Farms Vineyards and Winery, as the name implies, offers a fine selection of wine. It also has a 10 acre vineyard. But it is a unique place among Florida wineries. It's an actual small working farm.

"Green Eggs and Ham" is a best-selling and critically acclaimed book by Dr. Seuss, first published in 1960. It is one of the best selling children's books in history. Like many parents of the time, I read the book to my kids. Frankly, I hated the doggerel poems in the book, but the kids loved the words and begged for more.

The vineyards were planted in 1999, almost four decades after Dr. Seuss wrote the book. They also have large acreage in the Panhandle and get grapes from other growers in the Southeast.

The tie-in to Dr. Seuss's book (at least in my mind) is the 200 hens that free range under the canopy of the vineyard. These are American breed laying hens. Rhode Island Reds, Plymouth Barred Rocks and Aracaunas wander the property. The Aracuanas lay large green eggs. See the connection to Dr. Seuss?

The property boasts 10 acres of native southern muscadine and scuppernong grape varieties, a hydroponics growing system for strawberry production, and a highbush blueberry patch.

The centerpiece of this small working farm is the country store. It is built in the old fashioned Florida Cracker style. The building sits above the ground with a crawl space beneath. This is how almost all Florida buildings were constructed a century ago or less. The entrance is through sliding barn doors and a large open breezeway. Inside you will find many types of wine, homemade jams and jellies, sauces and syrups. Many gift baskets are also available.

Products in the store vary with the harvest season. Strawberry preserves, blueberry dressing, and jams and jellies are displayed on the tasting counter so you can try a sample. They even have eggs for sale, and raw honey from their own hives.

It's fun to browse the well-stocked store. It's also fun just to sit on the wide shady Florida Cracker porch and take in the sights.

Henscratch Farms offers a self-guided farm tour, and even gives you some Cheerios to feed the friendly hens as you wander around the property.

There are plenty of other things to do at Henscratch. You can pick your own strawberries from December through March. You can also attend grape stomping events. Private labels are available for your personally stomped wines.

There are also musical events from time to time. For example, during May blueberry season, they have a **"Blueberry Bluegrass Festival"**. For family reunions or larger events, Henscratch Farms has a nice open air pavilion with a kitchen.

A visit to Henscratch can also be coupled with a trip to nearby Lake **Placid** to see the fantastic downtown murals and find the schedule for the latest Caladium festival.

HOURS OF OPERATION
Henscratch Farms has a schedule that varies due to the harvest seasons.

December thru May
Tuesday – Saturday: 10:00 am - 5:00 pm
Sunday: 12:00 pm - 4:00 pm

June and July
Check the Henscratch website for special events.

August thru November
Tuesday – Saturday: 10:00 am - 4:00 pm
Sunday: 12:00 pm - 4:00 pm

HENSCRATCH FARMS LOCATION MAP

Hutchinson Farm Winery

8061 Stone Road
Apopka, Florida
Tel: 407-814-8330
Hutchinsonfarmwinery.com

Hutchinson Farm Winery is owned and operated by Sherry and John Hutchinson with the able assistance of two smart dogs who didn't bark at me. John goes by the nickname Duke and is a retired Physician's Assistant. Sherry is a nurse, but also worked for a time at a vineyard in New York State. They began to make wine for themselves in 2006. Their interest developed and soon they learned about **the Florida Grape Growers Association** and met a lot of people also interested in vineyards and making wine.

They learned about the art of growing grapes and making **Muscadine** and **Bunch** grape wines. These grapes were developed by university researchers in Florida. In 2007 they planted some acreage with Muscadine and Bunch grapes on the property that is now their vineyard and winery.

At first they just made wine for friends and family, but they got such good feedback they decided to start producing the wine commercially. And that's how the current operation was born in 2013. They quickly evolved from hobbyists to a real business.

In addition to wine from their own grapes, they import juice from California and Chile and make a blueberry wine from blueberry fields in nearby Ocoee.

The winery headquarters is in a small building with gifts and wine for sale and a small tasting counter. I recently tried the **wine tasting tour** and it was definitely worth it. I received a small sample of six from freshly opened bottles and enjoyed them all. Each taste was accompanied by a narrative from Sherry about the history of the wine, what it goes with and what they have tried to accomplish with the wines.

Most of the wines are not as sweet as those I've tasted at other Florida wineries. They are just sweet enough, but not too much. The wines I sampled were their White, Sweet White, Rose, Sweet Red, Red and Blue Darter Blueberry. They were all good, but I decided to buy a bottle of their Sweet White.

The winery is open **Thursday, Friday, Saturday** and **Sunday** from **Noon to 800pm** and sometimes a bit later.

To find the winery take County Road 435 south out of Apopka. When you go by the Clarcona Resort RV Park on your right, look for Stone Road on your left. A winery sign will alert you to

169

Stone Road from there just follow the signs along the narrow paved road.

HUTCHINSON FARM WINERY LOCATION MAP

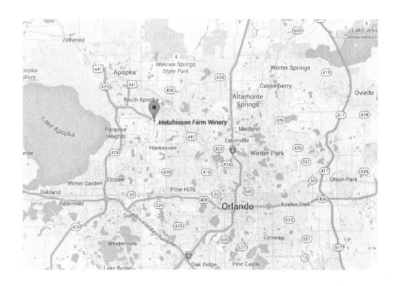

Lake Ridge Winery and Vineyards

19239 US-27 North
Clermont, Florida 347151
Tel: 800-768-WINE
Lakeridgewinery.com

Lakeridge Winery & Vineyards first popped into my life about 25 years ago. I drove each football weekend for many years from Orlando to Gainesville to watch the Florida Gators. In 1988 I noticed their beautiful Spanish style building under construction west of the turnpike north of Clermont. They opened for business not long after that in February 1989.

This comfortable place has become a very popular Orlando area attraction for tourists and residents alike in the years since they opened.

The beautiful main building and vineyards are on a 127-acre estate in the hilly country about 25 miles west of Orlando. Before the great freeze of 1982, these hills were covered with citrus groves.

The vineyard takes up 77 of the 127 acres, and includes Florida hybrid bunch grapes and varieties of Muscadines including Noble, Carlos and Welder.

Research on new varieties continues to be done in the vineyard. The staff engages in research along with the Florida Department of Agriculture. The winery has a large tasting room and a wonderful gift shop. Several types of wine are sold under the Lakeridge brands.

These wines can be purchased at many retail outlets in Florida. They are also set up for people interested in buying wine online.

In addition to all of their wines, the gift shop sells gourmet foods, cheeses, crackers, sauces and wine accessories. They can also put together one of the finest wine gift baskets in Florida. Surprise your friends with a nice gift basket.

There are probably more events held at this establishment than any of the other Florida wineries.

All year long there are arts and crafts shows, jazz concerts, harvest festivals, grape stomping events, vintage car shows and vintage music events. Complimentary tours and wine tastings are offered seven days a week. This is a fun place to visit even if you don't drink wine. The facility is also available for corporate parties, wedding receptions or any special occasions or events that need rented space.

HOURS OF OPERATION

Monday - Saturday: 10:00am - 5:00pm
Sunday: 11:00am - 5:00pm

LAKERIDGE WINERY LOCATION MAP

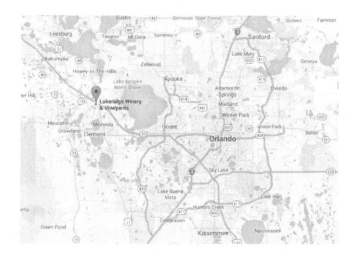

Whispering Oaks Winery

10934 County Rd 475
Oxford, Florida 34484
Tel: 352-748-0449
Winesofflorida.com

Whispering Oaks Winery is located on a large farm in the rolling countryside west of **The Villages** in an unincorporated area known as Oxford. They have 40,000 blueberry bushes on the farm, and naturally specialize in blueberry wines. The winery is fun to visit because of the enthusiastic personality of the owner, **Johannes Vanderwey**, and the ambience of the farm itself.

There is a friendly bar in the Visitor Center, and Johannes gives a tour of the wine making operation. Johannes came from Idaho a few years ago and has a farming and business background. After planting the blueberries, he operated the farm as a "you pick em" operation and also sold his berries to local markets. He wanted to make the farm self-sustaining; that's when the idea of a winery came to him.

He retained international wine expert **Dr. Brent Trela** to help him create his unique wine selection. Dr Trela is a hands on expert who is under contract with the winery and will have a lot to do with fine tuning their operation and helping develop new wines.

The winery has only been open since the winter of 2014, but has already attracted a large following of fans. The wine that is produced here is also available in many Florida stores including **Liquors of Ocala** and **Fresh Market** in The Villages, Orlando, Clearwater and Tampa.

Some Florida restaurants are also making the wine available. Some of these include **Ricciardis** in Brownwood; **Red Sauce, R.J. Gators** and **Garvino's** in Lake Sumter Landing; and **Mermaid Juice, Wine Cellars** and **The Wine Den** in Mount Dora.

The wines created by the winery range from sweet to dry, and they also have Sangria that is a blend of blueberry wine and citrus. The wines I tried while visiting were **Blushing Blueberry, Wildly Mild, Sensationally Sweet** and **Delightfully Dry**. All were blueberry wines and all were delicious. I also tried some Sangria and it was great too.

Johannes says there are two pounds of blueberries in every bottle of wine. Since blueberries are a well-known healthy antioxidant, even your doctor might approve of this particular alcoholic beverage.

There is entertainment on weekends at the winery. They have a beautiful shaded deck with a lovely pond and fountain waterfall that creates a great space for their entertainers and visitors. The temperature outside was 95 degrees when I visited but the outside deck was still comfortable.

Whispering Oaks Winery is open 7 days a week from 1100am to 700pm.

WHISPERING OAKS LOCATION MAP

FESTIVALS

Central Florida art festivals are held each year in many towns and cities of the region, including Orlando, Winter Park, Lake Buena Vista, Ocala, Winter Haven, Leesburg and Mount Dora. I have attended many festivals and art shows over my years in Florida, and have enjoyed every single one of them.

Here is a partial list of annual art festivals, art shows, folk festivals and other outdoor events in Central Florida arranged by month.

JANUARY (No art shows reported)

FEBRUARY

First Weekend
Mount Dora Arts Festival - Downtown Mount Dora

MARCH

First Weekend
Annual Original Highwaymen Weekend Extravaganza - Davenport

Second Weekend
Leesburg Fine Arts Festival - Leesburg

Third Weekend
Central Park Art Festival - Winter Haven

Fourth Weekend
Winter Park Sidewalk Art Festival - Winter Park

Final Weekend

Uptown Art Expo - Altamonte Springs

APRIL (No art shows reported)

MAY

Mother's Day Weekend
Mayfaire By The Lake - Lakeland (Lake Morton)

JUNE (No art shows reported)

JULY

Second Weekend
The Villages Craft Festival At Lake Sumter Landing - The Villages

AUGUST-SEPTEMBER (No art shows reported)

OCTOBER

Second Weekend
Authors Book Fair - Deltona

Annual Winter Park Autumn Art Festival - Winter Park

Third Weekend
Annual Mount Dora Bicycle Festival - Mount Dora

Fourth Weekend
Annual Mount Dora Craft Fair - Mount Dora

NOVEMBER

First Weekend
Lake Mary Heathrow Festival of Arts - Lake Mary

Horse Creek Festival & Florida Heritage Invitational Art Show - Davenport

Lake Eola Fall Fiesta In The Park - Orlando

Second Weekend
Festival Of The Masters - Lake Buena Vista

Weekend Before Thanksgiving
Longwood Arts & Crafts Festival - Longwood

Winter Garden Art Festival - Winter Garden

DECEMBER

First Weekend
Christmas Art Festival - Ocala

Orlando Pottery Festival - Orlando

HERITAGE AND HISTORY

Central Florida heritage and history begins with the early native Americans who dwelled in the area 12,000 years ago. The modern era was ushered in by three separate Seminole Wars.

Central Florida History

The forts that were built during the Seminole wars gave their names to many of the settlements in Central Florida. Fort King is now Ocala, Fort Gatlin is now Orlando, Fort Pierce is still Fort Pierce. Fort Drum, Fort Christmas, Fort Ogden, Fort Meade and other old forts are now either small villages or just place names in Florida history. They are still a large part of Central Florida heritage.

Many of the early settlers in Central Florida were pioneers who came down from Georgia and the Carolinas after the Civil War. The next big wave of people came after World War Two. The first settlers began arriving in Central Florida in the years just after the final Seminole War through the end of the Civil War.

Many of the pioneers began to homestead and start ranches in the prairie lands around Kissimmee, St. Cloud, Orlando and Ocala. In later years, they and other settlers planted citrus. Central Florida heritage is proud to have been the citrus and cattle capital of the world. The area led the world in citrus production until several freezes and epidemics of citrus canker devastated the groves and pushed the operations further south.

At one time Kissimmee was connected to the Gulf of Mexico near Fort Myers by a navigable waterway. Ships traveled along the Kissimmee River to Lake Okeechobee and west through the Caloosahatchee River. Kissimmee was a large port with many passenger and freight ships stopping by on a regular basis. Cattle and citrus were shipped out to ports around the world.

The Central Florida heritage of the cowboy is still very evident today in St. Cloud and Kissimmee. The annual Silver Spurs rodeo event is still a huge happening in these Central Florida Cracker towns.

The rural bucolic nature of Central Florida began to change when Martin Marietta built a huge defense plant in Orlando in the 1950's. The next big change was the development of Canaveral Air Station and Kennedy Space Center in Brevard County. These two projects had major impacts on Orlando's population. These huge endeavors are now part of Central Florida heritage.

The biggest changes of all came when Walt Disney World opened in October 1971. The population boomed and so did the traffic problems. The success of Disney encouraged other competitors to join in the fun and profit. Central Florida is now the location of the largest theme parks in Florida. Florida travel for most tourists includes visits to Walt Disney World, Universal Studios Florida and SeaWorld.

Central Florida heritage and history takes place in 9 counties that sprawl along the high sand ridge that is Florida's spine. This ridge was the beach in ancient times, and its surface is made of old rolling sand dunes. This large region starts between Ocala and Gainesville in the north, and extends south to the citrus country around Lake Placid and Sebring.

Ocala's rolling hills and pastures are known for producing some of the finest thoroughbred horses in the world. A wonderful Central Florida travel experience is to drive among the horse farms that surround Ocala.

The center part of this region, around Orlando and Clermont, was the citrus capital of the state until a big freeze changed things forever. Devastating freezes in Central Florida in the early 1980's destroyed many thousands of acres of groves. These old grove lands have been replaced in many cases by modern subdivisions.

Florida history has abundant examples of towns that thrived until their underlying resources were gone. Citrus and cypress boom towns are two examples. Walt Disney World, Universal Studios, SeaWorld and the other attractions transformed the area around Orlando into the sun and fun capital of the world.

Although Central Florida thrives on tourism, it is also the agricultural center of Florida. Oranges, grapefruit, tangerines, watermelon, peppers, tomatoes, celery and watercress are all grown in this area along the ridge and in the adjacent flatlands and valleys. Not so far south of Orlando you can still see cowboys at work in the vast pastures that range all the way down to Holopaw, Yeehaw Junction and beyond. These cowboys are a living reminder of Central Florida heritage.

Even with the population explosion around Orlando, the rural regions south of Kissimmee and St. Cloud still enjoy some of the quietest places in Florida. Orlando straddles I-4 and is the central anchor to the fast growing I-4 corridor. It is the major city in Central Florida. Since it is near the center of the State, many Floridians think it should be the state capital instead of Tallahassee.

US-27 is a major north-south four lane highway that meanders along the ridge part of the region. This is where some of the major citrus groves are located. The major tourist attractions in Orlando put a tremendous traffic load on I-4 and US-27. There are plenty of back roads in Orange County and surrounding counties that will help you avoid the traffic. Don't be afraid to explore and learn more about Central Florida heritage.

Central Florida Heritage Sites

Here is a list of 182 Central Florida heritage sites listed by county. The County Seat is also listed.

HARDEE: Wauchula

Main Street Wauchula

Paynes Creek Historic State Park

HIGHLANDS: Sebring

Archbold Biological Station
Avon Park Depot Museum
Avon Park Historic District
Highlands County Courthouse
Highlands Hammock State Park
Kenilworth Lodge
Old Lake Placid ACL Railroad Depot
Old Sebring Seaboard Airline Depot
Sebring Downtown Historic District
Sebring Fire Station
South Florida Community College Museum of Florida Art & Culture

LAKE: Tavares

Antique Boat Museum
Bowers Bluff Middens Archaeological District
Clermont Main Street, Inc.
Clermont Women's Club
Clifford House
Eustis Historic Museum
Eustis Main Street, Inc.
Ferran Park and the Alice B. McClelland Bandshell
First United Methodist Church
General James A. Van Fleet Trail State Park
Holy Trinity Episcopal Church
Kimball Island Midden Archaeological Site
Lake County Courthouse
Lake Griffin State Park

Lake Louisa State Park
Lakeside Inn
Lee Educational Center
Leesburg Downtown Partnership
Mote-Morris House
Mount Dora Chamber of Commerce
Mount Dora Lodge # 238, F&AM
Royellou Museum
Women's Club of Eustis

MARION: Ocala

Belleview City Hall
Citra United Methodist Church
Coca Cola Bottling Plant
Don Garlits Museum of Drag Racing and Museum of Classic
Automobiles
Dunnellon Boomtown Historic District
Dunnellon Main Street
Kerr City Historic District
Lake Lillian Neighborhood Historic District
Marion County Museum of History
Marion Hotel
McIntosh Historic District
McPherson Government Complex
Mount Zion AME Church
Ocala Amtrak Station
Ocala Historic Commercial District
Ocala Historic District
Old Fessenden Academy Historic District
Orange Springs Methodist Episcopal Church and Cemetery
Rainbow Springs State Park

Ritz Historic Inn
Silver River Museum and Environmental Education Center
Silver River State Park
Tuscawilla Park Historic District
West Ocala Historic District

ORANGE: Orlando

Albin Polasek House and Studio
All Saints Episcopal Church
Annie Russell Theatre
Apopka Historical Society
Cal Palmer Memorial Building
Carroll Building
Central Florida Railroad Museum
Cornell Fine Arts Museum
Eatonville Historic District
Fort Christmas Historical Park
Griffin Park Historic District
Harry P. Leu Gardens
Holocaust Memorial Resource and Education Center of Central Florida
Knowles Memorial Chapel
Lake Eola Heights Historic District
Lower Wekiva River Preserve State Park
Maitland Art Center
Maitland Historical Society and Museums
Moseley House
Nehrling Gardens and Museum
Ocoee Christian Church
Old Orlando Railroad Depot
Orange County Regional History Center

Rock Springs Run State Reserve
Rogers Building
Ryan Brothers, Inc.
St. George Greek Orthodox Church
Tinker Building
Tosohatchee State Reserve
Wekiwa Springs State Park
Well'sBuilt Museum of African American History and Culture
Windermere Town Hall
Winter Garden Downtown Historic District
Winter Garden Historic Residential District
Winter Park Historical Association and Museum
Withers-Maguire House Museum
Woman's Club of Winter Park
Zora Neale Hurston National Museum of Fine Arts

OSCEOLA: Kissimmee

Desert Inn
First United Methodist Church
Grand Army of the Republic Memorial Hall
Kissimmee Historic District
Old Holy Redeemer Catholic Church
Osceola County Courthouse
Osceola County Historical Museum and Pioneer Enrichment Center
St. Cloud Main Street, Inc.

POLK: Bartow

Auburndale Chamber - Mainstreet
Babson Park Woman's Club
Bartow Downtown Commercial District

Baynard House Museum

Beacon Hill-Alta Vista Residential District

Christ Church

City of Lake Wales

Clay Cut Centre

Cleveland Court Elementary School

Community Service Center of N.E. Polk County

Davenport Historic District

Dixieland Historic District

Downtown Bartow

Downtown Haines City Commercial District

Downtown Winter Haven Historic District

Dundee Depot Museum

East Lake Morton Residential District

First Baptist Church

Florida Air Museum

Florida Citrus Showcase

Florida Southern College Architectural District

Fort Meade Historic District

Frostproof City Hall

Frostproof Historical Society and Museum

Grand Hotel

Haines City Main Street

Henley Field Ball Park

Historic Bok Sanctuary

Homeland Heritage Park

Interlaken Historic Residential District

Lake Kissimmee State Park

Lake Mirror Promenade

Lake of the Hills Community Club

Lake Wales Art Center

Lake Wales Commercial Historic District
Lake Wales Historic Residential District
Landmark Baptist College
Lawton Chiles Middle Academy
Main Street Winter Haven, Inc.
Mobile Museum of Polk County
Mountain Lake Estates Residential District
Mulberry Phosphate Museum
Munn Park Historic District
North Avenue Historic District
Northeast Bartow Residential District
Oates Building
Old Lake Wales City Hall
Pinewood Estate
Polk County Historical Museum
Polk Theatre and Office Building
Pope Avenue Historic District
Roosevelt Academy
South Bartow Residential District
South Lake Morton Historic District
St. Mark's Episcopal Church
The Depot: Lake Wales Museum and Cultural Center
Water Ski Hall of Fame
West Area Adult School
Winston Elementary
Winter Haven Heights Historic Residential District
Woman's Club of Winter Haven

SEMINOLE: Sanford

Bradlee-McIntyre House
Florida Hotel

Geneva Museum and Historical Society
Geneva School House and Rural Heritage Center
Helen Stairs Theatre for the Performing Arts
Longwood Historic District
Museum of Seminole County History
Nelson and Company Historic District
Sanford Commercial District
Sanford Main Street, Inc.
Sanford Museum
Sanford Residential Historic District
Seminole County Student Museum, Center for the Social Studies
St. James AME Church

SUMTER: Bushnell

Dade Battlefield Historic Memorial
Dade Battlefield Historic State Park

You can use the Google search feature to find out more information about each of these sites.

A great historical novel that celebrates Central Florida heritage and history is **Patrick Smith's** classic work, **A Land Remembered.** It follows of lives of three generations of Florida pioneers.

DAY TRIPS

The Central Florida day trips recommended in this guide are designed to take you to off the beaten path to avoid the heavy traffic of the major theme parks. You will be in Old Florida once you get a fair distance away from the Interstate highways and toll roads.

I-4 is the east-west interstate in this region. It crosses the state of Florida from **Daytona Beach** through **Orlando** to **Tampa**.

Florida Turnpike is a major north-south toll road in this region. It starts in **Wildwood** south of **Ocala** and terminates in **Miami**. A branch of the Turnpike splits off north of Miami and heads south and east to Homestead on the way to the Florida Keys.

I-75 is another major north-south interstate in Central Florida. It crosses this region from **Ocala** in the north and heads south to **Tampa, Sarasota, Naples** and **Miami**.

The interstate exits are crowded with gas stations, fast food restaurants and motels. You can travel the state quickly and easily on these highways (except during rush hours), but not see much scenery or real towns as you will on my recommended Central Florida day trips.

The town signs you do see are usually a few miles from the downtown section. The fun begins when you get off the interstate and hookup with the less traveled roads. There are many state and county highways off the interstate that offer better scenery and a look at real towns. In Florida, some backroads are even four-laned. There are many well maintained city, county and state highways off the interstate that will show you better scenery and a look at real towns. Some of these backroads are even four laned.

The maps below show some of the Central Florida day trips that I recommend:

Winter Park to Orlando

Park Avenue from US-17/US-92 in Maitland south through **Winter Park** to the beautiful campus of **Rollins College** on the shore of Lake Virginia. Then meander along the residential streets on the lake shores south into **Orlando.** Beautiful old homes, sparkling blue lakes and green tree canopies. Great shopping and dining on brick paved Park Avenue in downtown Winter Park. One of my favorite central Florida day trips. About 12 miles.

Lake Buena Vista to Windermere

State Road 535 from **Lake Buena Vista** north to Chase Road, then east to **Windermere.** Old Florida houses, well maintained orange groves, crystal clear lakes and the pretty little tree shaded town of Windermere to enjoy lunch and strolling. Surrounded by gated communities that are home to the rich and famous. About 12 miles.

Orlando to Winter Haven

US-17 from **Orlando** to **Winter Haven** through **Kissimmee** and **Haines City**. Orange groves, small towns, big oak trees. Visit **Legoland** while you are in Winter Haven. About 47 miles.

Orlando to Mount Dora

US-441 from Orlando to **Mount Dora** through **Apopka**. Rolling country, great art galleries and shows in Mount Dora, and a large antique center at **Renningers**. About 27 miles.

Clermont to Lake Wales

US-27 from Clermont to **Lake Wales** through **Haines City**. Some congestion in the area where you cross I-4, but beautiful groves and rolling hills as you get south of the interstate. About 50 miles.

Lake Wales to Lake Placid

US-27 from **Lake Wales** to **Lake Placid** through **Avon Park and Sebring.** Interesting small towns, a large observation tower in Lake Placid (closed as of September 2010), and dozens of colorful murals on the commercial buildings in downtown Lake Placid. About 50 miles.

Mount Dora to Groveland

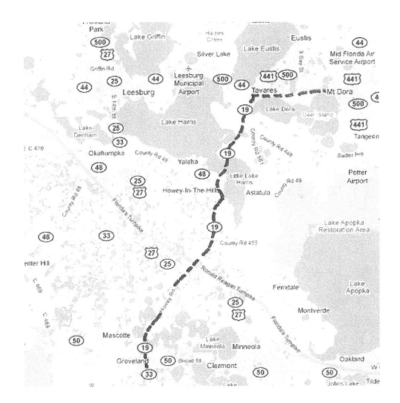

Old 441 from **Mount Dora** to **SR-19 in Tavares**. Then south through **Howey In The Hills** to **Groveland**. Rolling hills, old groves, little towns, art, antiques. Stop at **Boondockers** on Little Lake Harris in Howey In The Hills for a beer and good food. One of the nicest Central Florida day trips. About 26 miles.

Winter Haven to Wauchula

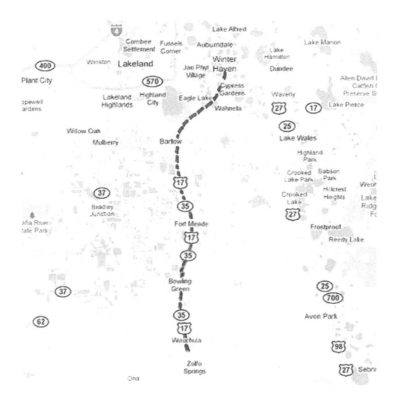

US-17 from Winter Haven to **Wauchula** through Bartow, **Fort Meade** and Bowling Green. Old Florida again, small towns, healthy little downtowns, many of them in the **Florida Main Street program**. About 36 miles.

Lake Wales to Frostproof

Old Scenic Highway 17 from Lake Wales south to **Frostproof** through **Highland Park** and **Babson Park**. Rolling groveland, heart of citrus country. The smell of orange blossoms in the spring will make you want to live in Florida forever. At least that's what happened to me more than a half century ago. About 14 miles.

Polk City to Auburndale

SR-559 from I-4 just south of **Polk City** to **Auburndale**. Rolling groveland and pretty little towns. Drive around the big lake in the heart of Auburndale and enjoy the old houses and the crystal clear waters. About 10 miles.

Mount Dora to The Villages Loop

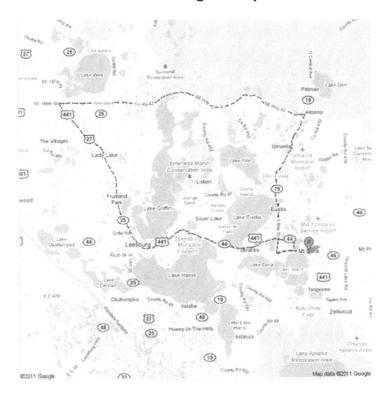

This trip starts from **Mount Dora** going west on Old US441 until it meets State Road 19. Take 19 through **Eustis** and **Umatilla** to **Altoona**, where you will turn west on State Road 42. Beautiful wooded rolling terrain along the south side of the Ocala National Forest. Take 42 all the way to US-27/441, then go south to **The Villages.** Stop in the main square for lunch, a drink, a concert, or all of those. Leave The Villages and continue south on US-441 all the way back to Mount Dora. About 60 miles.

Lady Lake to Weirsdale Loop

Leave US-441 at **Lady Lake**, go east and meander left until you reach **Lake Griffin Road**. Follow it all the way to where it ends at the **Harbor Hills** development. Turn left on dead end Matthews Rd and take a peek at an old Florida fish camp. Then go back to Lake Griffin Road and turn right on **Marion County Road**. Go north to tee intersection, then turn left. Go to SE 155th Ave and turn right (north). Go to State Road 42, then left to **Weirsdale,** south on State Road 25 back to Lady Lake. Rolling fields and hills, sparse development, neat old houses. The way Florida used to be and still is here. Next door to **The Villages Florida**.

Howey in the Hills to Yalaha Loop

Start in downtown **Howey-In-The-Hills**. Go west on Number 2 Rd to Bloomfield Ave, then north across State Road 48 to Lakeshore Drive. Follow Lakeshore along shore of Lake Harris. Turn left at old church built in 1875, then continue to Lime Ave and back to State Road 48. Follow State Road 48 back to Howey or take State Road 19 across the lake to Tavares. Rolling farmland, old houses, beautiful lake shore, old houses.

Orlando Day Trips

The Orlando Florida day trips and one tank trips described on Florida Backroads Travel are all within 100 miles of Orlando. Since Orlando is smack dab in the middle of Florida, there are many places you can go on the four corners of the compass.

We calculate that the average car can go at least 250 miles on a tank of gas. Many compact cars get a lot more than that. Your Orlando Florida day trips to the places mentioned on this website will leave you plenty of gas for exploring the back roads as well as visiting your destination.

The map below shows you some of the major cities within 100 miles of Orlando, and many of them are great destinations for Orlando Florida day trips.

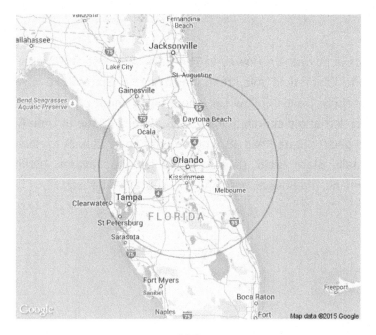

Avon Park is a small town along the scenic drive through citrus country south of Lake Wales.

Babson Park is also on the scenic drive through the citrus groves of central Florida, and is the home of Webber College.

Bok Tower Gardens is a botanical and architectural treasure near Lake Wales. The beautiful tower houses a carillon that plays at regular intervals.

Brevard Zoo is an animal habitat built entirely by volunteers and has become one of the most popular central Florida attractions.

Cherie Down Park has a beautiful beach in Cape Canaveral just north of Cocoa Beach. You can also visit Ron Jons, the Cocoa Beach Pier and other locat attractions.

Cocoa is a Space Coast town worth visiting because of its beautiful downtown area, Cocoa Village, noted for its fine restaurants and shopping.

Cross Creek was the home for many years of Marjorie Kinnan Rawlings, author of "The Yearling" and "Cross Creek".

Daytona Beach is motor city and beach city. You can drive on the hard packed sand beaches and visit the NASCAR facilities in town.

Deland is the home of Stetson University and has a wonderful downtown area with restaurants and shops in restored historic buildings. Lots of trees and murals throughout the town.

Doctor Phillips is a community south of Orlando along Sand Lake Road. It is loaded with many restaurants and shops, and is close to Universal Studios and the attractions along International Drive.

Eustis is an old Florida town northwest of Orlando that has a neat little downtown area and parks along the southeastern shore of Lake Eustis.

Evinston is a small community near Cross Creek and home to the old Wood & Swink General Store on the National Register of Historic Places.

Flagler Beachfront Winery is in Flagler Beach, right on the ocean. Enjoy wine tasting with an ocean view.

Florida Citrus Tower is a 65 year old attraction in Clermont west of Orlando. An elevator to the top takes you to a wonderful view of all central Florida.

Florida Museum of Natural History in Gainesville is the state's largest and is on the campus of the University of Florida.

Gainesville also has plenty to look at in addition to the university and the museums. The town has many historic neighborhoods and buildings, and a lot of nice restaurants.

Gatorland north of Kissimmee was entertaining tourists and locals long before Walt Disney World came on the scene.

Highlands Hammock State Park near Sebring is one of the finest examples of unspoiled natural Florida. Camping and day activities.

Highland Park is a small golf course town in the rolling hills south of Lake Wales. It has one of the oldest golf courses in Florida.

Lakeland is located among several lakes and has a lot of wonderful statuary to look at in downtown.

Lake Placid is the Caladium Capital of the World and has transformed its typical little downtown areas with murals on the buildings.

Lakeridge Winery is near Clermont. Watch wine being made, enjoy tasting and tours. Also lots of entertainment and music.

Lake Wales is the center of the citrus industry and is close to Bok Tower Gardens, a treat you should not miss.

Leu Gardens in Orlando has almost 50 acres of beautifully landscaped grounds, lakes and trails. Enjoy 200 year old oaks and acres of camelias.

Melbourne is on the Space Coast and Indian River Lagoon. Its downtown area is historic and renovated with lots of shops and restaurants.

Maytown Road is a lightly traveled paved road through one of Florida's last large wilderness areas.

Mount Dora is a small town on Lake Dora in the hill country northwest of Orlando. It has become an antique and art center with plenty of shops and frequent festivals and other events. It is one of our favorite Orlando Florida day trips.

New Smyrna Beach is where Orlando natives like to visit the beach. It is a charming small town along the Atlantic Ocean and Intracoastal Waterway.

Ocala is the center of the thoroughbred horse industry in Florida. A lot of great horse statues are scattered throughout downtown and the whole city is surrounded by beautiful rolling horse farms.

Orlando itself is loaded with more tourist attractions than one can possible visit. It also has many beautiful neighborhoods and a revitalized downtown business district. Get away from the bustle of Universal Studios and Walt Disney World and visit a real Florida city. Since the city is in the center of the state, it is the logical place to enjoy your Orlando Florida day trips.

Orlando Tree Tour is a self-guided tour of several significant trees in the City of Orlando, many of them hundreds of years old.

Orange County Regional History Center in Orlando has a lot of exhibits about the Orlando area that will entertain adults and kids alike.

SeaWorld Orlando is home to dolphins, whales, sharks and a lot of entertained tourists. One of the original big three Orlando attractions.

St. Augustine is one of Florida's favorite tourist attractions. Visit some of the oldest neighborhoods and buildings in the United States.

The Villages is a planned community northwest of Orlando that is developed around numerous golf courses. Lots of good dining and shopping.

Universal Studios Orlando is near SeaWorld and has a lot of shows and activities based on Universal movies. Islands of Adventure is loaded with thrill rides.

Vero Beach has some of the nicest beaches in Florida. Disney also has a beach resort just north of Vero in Wabasso.

Walt Disney World is the most visited theme park in the world. You can spend your entire vacation here, but you will pay dearly for it.

Webster flea markets are open only on Monday. The biggest flea market in Florida.

Windermere, a small town near Walt Disney World with canopied streets and Old Florida ambience.

Winter Garden, a small town west of Orlando with a revitalized downtown business district.

Winter Haven, a pretty town among the lakes south of Orlando. The home of Legoland on the grounds of the former Cypress Gardens.

Winter Park, a small upscale enclave in the Orlando metro area on the north side. Great shopping, dining and art festivals. Morse Museum with a lot of Tiffany objects, and Rollins College.

EPILOGUE

Mike Miller has lived in Florida since 1960. He graduated from the University of Florida with a degree in civil engineering and has lived and worked in most areas of Florida. His projects include Walt Disney World, EPCOT, Universal Studios and hundreds of commercial, municipal and residential developments all over the state.

During that time, Mike developed an understanding and love of Old Florida that is reflected in the pages of his website, **Florida-Backroads-Travel.com**. The website contains several hundred pages about places in Florida and things to do. The information on the website is organized into the eight geographical regions of the state.

Central Florida Backroads Travel is based on the website. It is the second in what will be a series of eight regional guides that can be downloaded in PDF format or purchased as Amazon

Kindle books. If you find any inaccuracies in this guide, including restaurants or attractions that have closed, please contact Mike at Florida-Backroads-Travel.com and let him know. It is his intention to update the guide periodically and publish updated editions.

If you have enjoyed this book and purchased it from Amazon, Mike would appreciate it if you would take a couple of minutes to post a short review at Amazon. Thoughtful reviews help other customers make better buying choices. He reads all of his reviews personally, and each one helps him write better books in the future. Thanks for your support!

BOOKS BY MIKE MILLER

Florida Backroads Travel
Northwest Florida Backroads Travel
North Central Florida Backroads Travel
Northeast Florida Backraods Travel
Central East Florida Backroads Travel
Central Florida Backroads Travel
Central West Florida Backroads Travel
Southwest Florida Backroads Travel
Southeast Florida Backroads Travel
Florida Everglades
Florida Wineries
Florida Festivals
Florida Carpenter Gothic Churches
Florida One Tank Trips, Volume 1
Florida Heritage Travel, Volumes I, II, III
Living Aboard a Boat
Florida Wineries

Made in the USA
Coppell, TX
22 July 2025

52225319R00125